I0754113

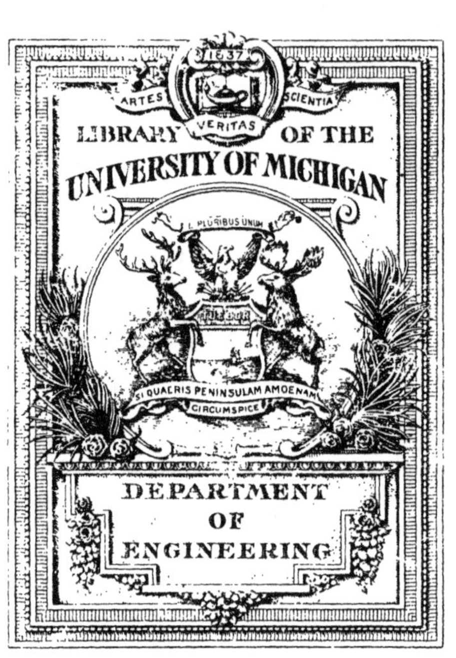
1837
ARTES
SCIENTIA
VERITAS
LIBRARY OF THE
UNIVERSITY OF MICHIGAN
E PLURIBUS UNUM
SI QUAERIS PENINSULAM AMOENAM
CIRCUMSPICE
DEPARTMENT
OF
ENGINEERING

STREET-CLEANING

AND THE DISPOSAL OF A CITY'S WASTES: METHODS AND RESULTS AND THE EFFECT UPON PUBLIC HEALTH, PUBLIC MORALS, AND MUNICIPAL PROSPERITY

STREET-CLEANING

AND THE DISPOSAL OF A CITY'S WASTES: METHODS AND RESULTS AND THE EFFECT UPON PUBLIC HEALTH, PUBLIC MORALS, AND MUNICIPAL PROSPERITY

BY

GEORGE E. WARING, JR.,

COMMISSIONER OF STREET-CLEANING IN THE CITY OF NEW YORK

NEW YORK
DOUBLEDAY & McCLURE CO.
1898

THIS BOOK IS DEDICATED

TO

WILLIAM L. STRONG

MAYOR OF NEW YORK

TO WHOSE EARNEST SUPPORT SUCCESS IN MY DEPARTMENT

HAS BEEN SO LARGELY DUE

CONTENTS

LIST OF ILLUSTRATIONS

CHAPTER I

HISTORY

UP to 1881 the cleaning of the streets of New York was under the charge of a bureau of the Police Department. There is little to be found in the city's records as to the manner in which the work was done, but it was evidently very unsatisfactory to the people.

In 1881 the Department of Street-Cleaning was created by law, and Mr. James S. Coleman was made the first commissioner, being appointed by the mayor, with the approval of the Board of Health. He held the office for nearly nine years. In 1882 he let out the cleaning of the streets south of Fourteenth Street to contractors, doing the work north of that street with his own forces. The contract system was continued through nearly his whole term. He said:

"Broadway below Fourteenth Street is not included in the contractors' districts. Nominally it is cleaned partly by the city and partly by the Broadway and Seventh Avenue Railroad Company, the charter of the latter obliging it to clean that portion of the roadway which lies between the car-tracks and within two feet of them on either side; the Department of Street-Cleaning has charge of the remainder. As a matter of fact, however, the whole work is done under a special agreement whereby the possibly conflicting and complicated double work by the railroad company and the department is avoided." This contract is still maintained.

In Mr. Coleman's report of 1889 he speaks of numerous aggravating impediments to good work, many of which still exist. Laws and ordinances seemed to have had no effect on the people. Mr. Coleman says: "A good deal of time might be employed in the enumeration of culpable acts and shameful delinquencies on the part of the merchants and householders. It has frequently happened that the street-sweeping machine has passed down the street, and before it has reached the nearest corner men and women have been seen deliberately emptying receptacles full of refuse and rubbish from their shops or residences upon the pavements just swept. Handbills and other printed matter distributed to pedestrians were thrown on the sidewalk or street. . . . Such things were not done, perhaps, because the offenders had resolved to be blameworthy and contemptuous, but because they were imbued with the spirit of indifference to the public welfare and had long been accustomed to do such things without fear of the law." He estimated that there were "close to fifty thousand" vehicles in the streets, while the law regulating the deposit of building-material and rubbish was notoriously disregarded. Gutters were obstructed by such material, stopping flowage and causing pools of stagnant water to stand on the street.

Mr. Horace Loomis held the office of commissioner from January 17, 1890, until April 4 of the same year,

THE ANNUAL PARADE.

FOREMEN AND PLATOONS OF SWEEPERS READY FOR THE MARCH.

This picture is from a photograph taken at the first parade of the New York Street-Cleaning Department. The effect of the parade was to stimulate and encourage the men, and to increase the respect of citizens for these city employees.

when Mr. Hans S. Beattie was appointed. He was succeeded by Mr. Thomas S. Brennan, September 17, 1891.

In 1892 the department was entirely reorganized, as the result of a careful investigation of the whole subject made by a committee appointed by Mayor Grant. Mr. Brennan was reappointed under this law. He was succeeded by Mr. William S. Andrews, July 21, 1893, and he by the writer, January 15, 1895.

The report of Mayor Grant's committee is very full and instructive. It shows practically that the department was not efficiently managed, and gives ample details as to its defects. The committee reached the following general conclusion: "With good labor, skilfully organized and properly superintended, the streets can unquestionably be kept clean. With labor employed on the present methods, no organization, however skilful, and no superintendence, however faithful, can produce entirely satisfactory results."

After reciting the laws and ordinances, the committee expressed its opinion that New York should be one of the cleanest cities in the world. "Practically it is one of the dirtiest, because they are so habitually violated and so feebly enforced as to become dead letters."

Concerning the cost of the work it is said that "this sum of more than a million and a quarter of dollars, however, by no means represents the total amount expended for street-cleaning and removing refuse. It is well known that many householders, in order to secure clean streets in front of their premises, employ private street-cleaners; others employ private ashmen to take their ash-barrels from within the gate under the stoop, so as to avoid putting the ashes out in front of the house; and still others fee the public ashman to perform this service—a practice which, it is stated, makes the position of ashman on certain routes much sought after."

This committee set forth with emphasis the serious objections to the universal practice of standing trucks in the streets.

It also conducted an experiment in the sweeping of a certain district by the "block system." This portion of its report is worthy of very careful consideration, because it resulted in the adoption of the system now in vogue.

The reports of Commissioner Coleman and of Mayor Grant's committee are copiously quoted in the Appendix, and those readers who are interested in anything like a careful study of the subject will find reference thereto most important.

The more recent history of the department and its operations relates to the conditions existing immediately prior to the inauguration of Mayor Strong and to what it has since done. This is given in the following chapters relating to specific branches of the subject.

CHAPTER II

CONDITIONS UNDER RECENT ADMINISTRATIONS

HAVING thus stated the prominent historical facts in connection with the Department of Street-Cleaning of New York, attention will now be given to the conditions which obtained under the administration of the new law of 1892, this being during the last fourteen months of the administration of Commissioner Brennan and all of that of Commissioner Andrews, or from May 9, 1892, to January 15, 1895, when the control of the work fell to me.

The very unsatisfactory condition of the streets, and the demoralization of the department at that time, were, and still are, matters of notoriety. The character and the causes of this condition are sufficiently shown in the preceding chapter.

The kernel of it all lies in the fact, especially set forth by Commissioner Beattie, that men were not employed for work in the Department of Street-Cleaning because they were suitable for the work, but because their appointment was urged by politicians and for political reasons.

IN FRONT OF NO. 9 VARICK PLACE, MARCH 17, 1893.

a

THE SAME STREET, MAY 29, 1895.

b

The necessary result of such a state of affairs appeared very fully in the illustrated description of the condition of the streets, and of the degree of their encumbrance and their neglect, made by a committee of the City Club, with a view to securing the removal of Commissioner Brennan for neglect of duty.

A large number of photographs were taken, showing the condition of the streets in March, 1893, and affidavits were published, describing the manner in which the work of street-cleaning was done and neglected.

Two of these are reproduced here, in contrast with photographs of the identical spots taken the end of May, 1895.

Such illustrative contrasts might be duplicated for the entire collection of the City Club, for every block in New York is now as clean as those shown here. The condition of the streets as photographed in 1893 was further set forth in the accompanying affidavits, which testify to the inefficiency of the department at that time. These affidavits are very voluminous, and they relate to some hundreds of different points.

The photographs were taken at a time when the snow and ice had not entirely melted, and due allowance is to be made for this.

The following are some of the descriptions set forth in the affidavits:

"Opposite No. 379 [East Fourth Street] there was about a ton of ashes, garbage, old cloth, tin cans, and five old barrels. . . . In front of Nos. 344 and 346 there were seven barrels, refuse overflowing all over the sidewalks. . . . The general condition of this street was bad. I have enumerated the most filthy places; but all along the street it has the appearance of being the dumping-ground of the whole ward.

"This street [Pitt Street] was also very dirty; mud, ashes, filth, and garbage lay all over it to the depth of about eight inches.

"On Ludlow Street, from the corner of Stanton, the street is very filthy. Trucks, wagons, and carts were standing in filth of every kind from one to two feet deep, and the street was covered with old paper, rags, ashes, garbage, straw, and general refuse.

"On the west side of Thompson Street, from Houston Street north, were piles of snow, ice, mud, garbage, and general filth, from three to four feet high, on which trucks and wagons were piled. Opposite nearly every door there were overflowing barrels of refuse. On Sullivan Street, from Houston to Bleecker, barrels of ashes and garbage were in front of nearly every door; and along the side of the street piles of garbage, old rags, tins, oyster-shells, old paper, and general refuse, from two to four feet high, from which a bad stench arose.

"On Bedford Street, in front of No. 139, were two barrels of refuse on the sidewalk, and about three barrels more dumped around them. . . . This street was dirty all along. I have specified the worst places only.

"A man named Calder, of 688 Washington Street, volunteered the information that the ashman had not been there for six weeks.

"The whole block [in Greenwich Street] was in as bad a condition throughout, and twenty-one trucks were stationed upon it. In No. 395 a woman informed me that ashes had only been taken away twice in two weeks. The box in front of this house has the refuse of four houses dumped into it, and she said it should be emptied at least three times a week to keep the refuse from being

MORTON STREET, CORNER OF BEDFORD, LOOKING TOWARD BLEECKER STREET, MARCH 17, 1893.

c

THE SAME STREET, MAY 29, 1895.

scattered over the walk. At this time a heap of ashes lay in front of the house on the street.

"There was a pile of garbage in front of Van Holten & Bay's store at 500 Ninth Avenue. A clerk in the store said that people had to dump the garbage in the gutters, because the carts of the Street-Cleaning Department did not take it away. He could not remember the last time the block was cleaned."

I remember, as a characteristic incident, that a few days after my appointment I drove down-town with my wife, and passed through Elizabeth Street, which was no worse than most other obscure streets of the city. She begged me to resign at once and go back to Newport, saying, "It is utterly hopeless. You surely can never clean Elizabeth Street; you will only disgrace yourself by trying to do it." This street was lined on both sides at midday with unharnessed trucks; the sidewalks were thick with overflowing ash and garbage receptacles; black mud was several inches deep in the street, and the sidewalks themselves were slimy with the filth tracked on to them from the crossings. The people had a squalid and hopeless air, and the outlook was certainly very discouraging. The same condition prevailed throughout the more densely peopled quarters, and even in the relatively quiet and respectable streets running from Bleecker Street toward the North River there was little evidence that systematic cleaning had been carried on for a long time.

I have no knowledge of the methods prevailing under the predecessors of Commissioner Andrews; but I do know that he had done the best that he could, under his limitations, to improve the situation. The department still feels, and always will feel, the influence of his intelligence and zeal in the theoretical part of his work. He secured the passage of several amendments to the law organizing the department which are of the greatest value—amendments which could be obtained now only by an influential Republican politician, and without which good work would be almost impossible.

He told me during my tutelage many things confirmatory of what is said in the following chapter as to the effect of political control. He had been promised absolute independence in the matter of appointments and dismissals. He very early found it necessary to dismiss an important member of the clerical force, whose habits made him practically worthless. He immediately felt the weight of a higher authority, and was told, "So-and-so is my man; you must take him back." He did take him back, and he took a back seat from that time forward. I have recently been told by a stable foreman, who is a "hold-over from Tammany times," and who is a most excellent and efficient officer, that it was absolutely impossible to get work properly done under the old régime. For example, a man had been sent to him to be put "on the floor," meaning that he was to be used as a general utility man about the stable. The foreman found him inefficient, and told him he must go to work. The man replied, "I did n't come here to work." He was reported at once for dismissal, and was suspended. He returned the next day, reinstated and irremovable.

I could give a hundred instances of similar cases, but the above are sufficient. Reasoning backward, one could now reconstruct, by restoring the former methods, the same horrible condition of the streets that then existed. That condition was a natural consequence of the stultifying of the efforts of any commissioner by the superior power of ward politicians and their superiors. The streets of the city are now measurably clean—cleaner than they have ever been before; but if the hands of the commissioner and his staff were tied by the absolute destruction of discipline which political control must give, they would relapse into their former condition within three months.

The records show that at the end of Commissioner Andrews's term the uniformed force consisted of the following: 1 general superintendent, 1 assistant superintendent, 11 district superintendents, 58 foremen, 1275 sweepers, 908 drivers. As to the plant, there were 684 horses, 619 carts and trucks, 87 sprinkling-wagons, and 76 sweeping-machines.

CHAPTER III

THE EFFECT OF POLITICAL CONTROL AS SHOWN BY THE CONDITION OF THE DEPARTMENT AT THE BEGINNING OF THE PRESENT ADMINISTRATION

THE tendency to ascribe former defects of the Department of Street-Cleaning in New York City to one political party, as such, seems to me not to be fair. I had this prevailing tendency myself when I first took office; but experience has taught me that it was a question, not of party, but of politics. I have no reason now to suppose that matters would have been in any wise better had the other party been in control of the city government. Whatever may be the differences of their members in avocation or in attainments, when it is a question of the government of the city by the spoilsmen for the party, there is nothing to choose between political organizations.

I am, to this extent, no more an anti-Tammany man than I should be an anti-Republican man if Republicans had brought about the same defects had their party been in power. In describing the former condition of the streets and of the department, I am making no criticism of Tammany Hall, only of politics as the ruling factor in city government. The improved present condition could not have been brought about without an absolute disregard of all political considerations in the management of the business. My work has succeeded because it has been done for its own sake alone. The same success awaits any competent man who will manage any other of the city departments on the same principle.

If the whole city is ever so managed the people will be glad.

Whatever the cause, no one will now question that the former condition of the streets was bad—very bad. No one can question the truth of the following description:

Before 1895 the streets were almost universally in a filthy state. In wet weather they were covered with slime, and in dry weather the air was filled with dust. Artificial sprinkling in summer converted the dust into mud, and the drying winds changed the mud to powder. Rubbish of all kinds, garbage, and ashes lay neglected in the streets, and in the hot weather the city stank with the emanations of putrefying organic matter. It was not always possible to see the pavement, because of the dirt that covered it. One expert, a former contractor of street-cleaning, told me that West Broadway could not be cleaned, because it was so coated with grease from wagon-axles; it was really coated with slimy mud. The sewer inlets were clogged with refuse. Dirty paper was prevalent everywhere, and black rottenness was seen and smelled on every hand.

The practice of standing unharnessed trucks and wagons in the public streets was well-nigh universal in all except the main thoroughfares and the better residence districts. The Board of Health made an enumeration of vehicles so standing on Sunday, counting twenty-five thousand on a portion of one side of the city; they reached the conclusion that there were in all more than sixty thousand. These trucks not only restricted traffic and made complete street-cleaning practically impossible, but they were harbors of vice and crime. Thieves and highwaymen made them their dens, toughs caroused in them, both sexes resorted to them, and they were used for the vilest purposes, until they became, both figuratively and literally, a stench in the nostrils of the people. In the crowded districts they were a veritable nocturnal hell. Against all this the poor people were powerless to get relief. The highest city officials, after feeble attempts at removal, declared that New York was so peculiarly constructed (having no alleys through which the rear of the lots could be reached) that its commerce could not be carried on unless this privilege were given to its truckmen; in short, the removal of the trucks was "an impossibility."

There was also some peculiarity about New York which made it inevitable that it should have dirty streets. Other towns might be clean, but not this one. Such civic pride as existed had to admit these two unfortunate drawbacks.

The average annual death-rate from 1882 to 1894, inclusive, was 25.78 per thousand persons living—equal to more than fifty thousand deaths in the year on the basis of the present population. Eye and throat diseases due to dust, and especially to putrid dust, were rife. No effort was made to remove snow for the comfort of the people, only for the convenience of traffic. But little more than twenty miles of streets were cleared after a snow-storm. As a result, the people, especially the poorer people who could not change their wet clothing and could not buy rubber shoes, suffered to an alarming degree from colds and their results.

The department itself was such as its work would indicate. Like all large bodies of men engaged in any stated duty, its force had much good material, but it was mainly material gone to waste for lack of proper control. It was hardly an organization; there was no spirit in it; few of its members felt secure in their positions; no sweeper who was not an unusually powerful political worker knew at what moment the politician who had got him his place would have him turned out to make room for another. A ledger account of patronage was kept with each Assemb'y district, and district leaders are even said to have had practically full control of the debit and credit columns, so that they could deposit a dismissal and check out an appointment at will. Useful service can be had from no force thus controlled.

Nearly every man in the department was assessed for the political fund. I have seen an order, signed by one of my predecessors, practically directing every sweeper and driver to pay to the chief clerk a certain percentage of each week's pay. This was to be used for "political" purposes—how or by whom or for whom was not stated. The working-men of the force generally were in a miserable condition; they were the objects of ridicule and scorn, and they knew it. They did such work as they were compelled to do, and, as a rule, they did no more. Nominally, they wore a uniform, but they were not distinguished by it. The district superintendents and foremen, as a rule, either could not exercise effective control over their men, or they did not take the trouble to do so. Nothing was done *with a will;* the organization, as a whole, was a slouch.

The stock and plant were what they might have been expected to be under these conditions. In some of the stables there was not even an extra set of cart-harness, and some that were in use were mended by the drivers, on the streets, with bits of wire and string. Disorder and demoralization were the rule.

This is a severe condemnation of a department that spent $2,366,419.49 in a year (in 1894), as against $2,776,-749.31 in 1896, and did ineffective work with it; but it is just. The condition of the streets, of the force, and of the stock was the fault of no man and of no set of men. It was the fault of the system. The department was throttled by partizan control—so throttled it could neither do good work, command its own respect and that of the public, nor maintain its material in good order. It was run as an adjunct of a political organization. In that capacity it was a marked success. It paid fat tribute; it fed thousands of voters, and it gave power and influence to hundreds of political leaders. It had this appointed function, and it performed it well.

When I took charge of the department I found the district superintendents and foremen more or less uniformed. Few, if any, of them wore the complete uniform, and still fewer had a promising look. They seemed to be an easy-going, happy-go-lucky set of men, who had made up their minds that it was not possible to improve the state of affairs, and who had learned to make the best of the situation. The sweepers wore a sort of brownish suit, save when they found it more convenient to wear something else, and, pretty generally, grayish-brown caps with the letters "D. S. C." on the front. They kept their tools at home, in cellars under saloons, in yards behind corner groceries, in livery stables, or wherever else they could get permission to store them. Their roll-calls were at the street-corner or on the gutter. They had no habitation, and they seemed hardly fit to have a name.

Commissioner Andrews had inaugurated a system of section stations, by which the men of each two sections adjoining would have a place of meeting and storage-room for their tools in a room of their own; but this custom had by no means become general at the time when he left office. The stables were ill kept and disorderly, and were largely the resort of friendly idlers of the neighborhood.

It is hardly necessary to extend this description. The only thing that could be said in favor of it was that it was quite uniform in its lack of uniformity. There was little evidence of a controlling central authority.

As I have since had ample occasion to learn, very many of the officers, and of the men as well, were first-rate material, who needed only proper guiding to become effective. In fact, it is not too much to say that the best of the workmen and some of the best of the officers of to-day were among those described above.

There seems to have been no effort made to restrain the tendency for drink, which was conspicuous, especially among the drivers. Dismissals in the working-force for gross drunkenness were, of course, frequent; but a man could safely drink pretty steadily throughout the day without endangering his position. The neighborhood of the various dumps to which the drivers take their loads of refuse used to be specially valuable as sites for the liquor traffic. One owner tells me that in 1894 opposite one of the dumps he had four saloon-keeper tenants, whose rents ranged from eleven hundred to fifteen hundred dollars per annum. There is now only one of these saloons left open, and that pays a rental of only four hundred dollars per annum.

My early acquaintance with the department was not without its amusing incidents. I found, for example, that the general superintendent had an unusual capacity for handling the roughly organized force employed in the removal of snow. He had been reported to me as a Tammany captain, and as one of the chief agencies through which his political organization had worked the department. He was strongly recommended for dismissal. Remembering the wise injunction "not to swap horses when crossing a stream," I waited until the snow season had passed. I then sent for him, and told him that he had been represented as a "rank Tammany man," etc.

He said with mild submission, "Whenever you want my resignation, it is at your service." I said, "Don't be quite so fast; let me hear your version of your case." He said, "Do you know what a Tammany man is? It is a man who votes for his job. I have been a Tammany man, and a faithful one. I have worked for the organization; I have paid regular contributions to it. But I am a Waring man now." He probably saw an unexplained smile on my face, for he said, "Don't misunderstand me. If Tammany comes into power again I shall be a Tammany man again." This frankness met its reward, and I have had the great advantage of Mr. William Robbins's active and earnest assistance from that day to this, and I trust to have it for many a long day yet.

CHAPTER IV

THE REORGANIZATION OF THE FORCE

I ACCEPTED the commissionership of street-cleaning with the positive assurance of Mayor Strong that I should not be interfered with in the matter of appointments and dismissals, and that I should "have my own way" generally. His power to dismiss me is unlimited, and he could get rid of me any day if I did not suit him; but so long as I should remain I was to be the real head of my department. The mayor has lived up to his promise from that day to this. I have sometimes been a sore trial to him, especially in my relations with certain pensioners and labor leaders, and he has wished he might wash his hands of me more than once; but he saw reasons for bearing with my conduct until the storm blew over. He has never tried to influence me in the matter of "patronage," nor has he ever insisted on controlling the policy of my work. If he had done otherwise the result would not have been the same.

At the outset the employees of the department expected to be turned out, as a matter of course. Their positions were spoils which belonged to the victors, and they were filled with apprehension as to their future bread and butter. They knew the public would not longer put up with unclean streets, and that the clean sweeping demanded might properly begin with them.

Knowing that organizations of men are good or bad according to the way in which they are handled, that "a good colonel makes a good regiment," I paid attention first to those at the top—to the colonels. I found the general superintendent to be an excellent man for his duties, while most of the others were from very indifferent to decidedly bad. These were got rid of. In filling their places I sought men mainly with military training or with technical education and practice, not one of whom had any political alliance which he was not willing to sever. They were nearly all young men.

When the important offices had been filled attention was turned to the rank and file of the working-force. The men were assured that their future rested solely with themselves; that if they did their work faithfully and well, kept away from drink, treated citizens civilly, and tried to make themselves a credit to the department, there was no power in the city that could get them out of their places, so long as I stayed in mine. On the other hand, if they were drunkards, incompetent, blackguards, or loafers, no power could keep them in. When they found that I really meant what I said—and it took them some time to get such a strange new idea into their heads—they took on a new heart of hope, and turned their eyes to the front. From that day their improvement has been constant and most satisfactory. Their white uniforms, once so derided, have been a great help to them, and they know it; and the recognition of the people has done still more for them. Indeed, the parade of 1896 marked an era in their history. It introduced them to the prime favor of a public by which, one short year before, they had been contemned; and the public saw that these men were proud of their positions, were self-respecting, and were the object of pride on the part of their friends and relatives who clustered along their line of march.

What has really been done has been to put a man instead of a voter at the other end of the broom-handle. The "White Wings" are by no means white angels, but they are a splendid body of men, a body on which the people of New York can depend for any needed service, without regard to hours or personal comfort. A trusted sweeper, for example, will stand on a windy dock-log all night long, and night after night, protecting the city against the wiles and tricks of the snow-carters. He gets no extra pay for this, but his extra service and his hardship are compensated by the consciousness that he is doing good work, that his good work is appreciated by his officers, and that the force to which he belongs is winning public favor partly because of what he himself is doing. In other words, the whole department is actuated by a real *esprit de corps*, without which no organization of men can do its best, either in war or in peace.

The discipline is rigid and uniform. It is regulated and enforced according to these rules, which are posted in all section stations and stables:

The following abstract of the offenses of drivers and sweepers in the department, and the penalties prescribed therefor, is published for the information and guidance of all concerned. Hereafter any offense will be reported (on the prescribed form and in the existing manner, through the stable foreman in the case of drivers, and through the section foreman, approved by the district superintendent, in the case of sweepers) as a first, second, third, or fourth violation of Rule....., and the recommendation for punishment must not *exceed* the code of penalties.

When the prescribed penalty is dismissal, the offender may be suspended without pay, awaiting the action of the commissioner. A fourth violation of rules, of whatever character, will indicate that the man is incorrigible, and he may be dismissed.

Except in the case of men recommended for dismissal, there will be no suspensions. The punishment will be forfeiture of pay, and men who refuse to work while subject to such forfeiture will be at once dismissed.

This order will be posted on the bulletin boards at stables and section stations, and every employee of the department will be assumed to understand it.

Explanation: "D" means dismissal. 1, 2, 3, 5, and 10 mean the forfeiture of so many days' pay.

Rule	CHARACTER OF OFFENSE	PENALTY Offense 1st	2d	3d	4th
1.	Absence for more than five days without authority of the commissioner	D			
2.	Failure to report or send notice to foreman when sick	1	3	D	
3.	Absence from roll-call at proper hour	1	2	3	D
4.	Failure to return to stable or section station promptly after work is over and reporting time to stable foreman, section foreman, or clerk	2	3	5	D
5.	Failure to provide himself with the prescribed uniform, oilskin suits, sweater, and badge after reasonable time	D			
6.	Failure to wear prescribed uniform and badge while on duty in the manner directed by orders	3	D		
7.	Neglect to keep uniform and cap in neat condition	1	2	3	D
8.	Failure to keep horse, harness, cart, machine, etc., in good order, and failing to report injury to them to foreman at once	1	3	5	D
9.	Driving, using, or interfering with any horse, cart, harness, machine, etc., not assigned to him by proper authority, without good reason	1	3	5	D
10.	Neglecting or abusing a horse, whipping or striking a horse, using a horse which is sick or lame, and failing to take such horse to stable or reporting him to foreman	D			
11.	Neglecting to adjust harness properly while at work	1	3	5	D
12.	Neglecting to have lost shoes replaced on horse at nearest department stable as soon as practicable	1	3	5	D
13.	Leaving cart, etc., and horse unattended in street without good reason	1	3	5	D
14.	Failure to feed horse properly during swing	D			
15.	Failure to water horse properly during work hours	D			
16.	Failure to remove bits and to dump carts while feeding at noon	5	D		
17.	Deliberately trotting or galloping a horse	5	10	D	
18.	Failure properly to care for horse, harness, cart, etc., before leaving stable after return from work	D			
19.	Loitering at work	2	5	D	

Rule	CHARACTER OF OFFENSE	PENALTY Offense 1st	2d	3d	4th
20.	Failure to clean up his route or area of streets assigned, properly, by reason of neglect or loafing	3	5	D	
21.	Failure or refusal to obey orders of superiors	D			
22.	Having a helper or conductor with him without authority	D			
23.	Sorting over or picking over refuse or permitting others so to do	D			
24.	Neglecting to pick up and remove small stones found on route, and failing to report large ones or other obstructions lying in the street, such as gutter-planks, etc., to section foreman	1	3	5	D
25.	Taking up anything but ashes, garbage, and street-sweepings, except where they are mixed in small quantities in a receptacle or ash-barrel	2	5	D	
26.	Removing the contents of more than one receptacle so mixed, from one place, and neglecting to report such condition to section foreman	2	5	D	
27.	Mixing ashes and garbage together in districts where it is forbidden	5	D		
28.	Neglecting to report to district superintendents, stable foremen, or section foremen, where suitable receptacles are not provided, where they are improperly filled, and where refuse is spilled on sidewalks or streets	3	5	D	
29.	Neglecting to keep load covered and allowing it to blow or spill on street	3	D		
30.	Failing to have cart number exposed	3	5	D	
31.	Failing to provide himself with the proper implements to perform the work assigned him	1	3	5	D
32.	Accepting or demanding a fee or gratuity for work done	D			
33.	Entering a liquor saloon during work hours	3	D		
34.	Being under the influence of liquor while on duty	D			
35.	Using abusive or threatening language to a superior	D			
36.	Failing to turn over his dump ticket at end of day's work to foreman or clerk at stable	3	D		
37.	Failure to report promptly defects in brooms or mechanism of machines to foreman	1	3	5	D
38.	Neglect of driver or sweeper to water street properly to lay the dust	3	5	D	
39.	Using machine before street is sprinkled	D			
40.	Neglect to close hydrant after use	2	5	D	
41.	Failing to report change of residence to foreman	5	10	D	
42.	Removing improper material	5	10	D	
43.	Being boisterous or using profane language or any incivility to citizens	1	3	5	D
44.	Failure to keep gutters and culverts clear and clean	1	2	3	D
45.	Failure to keep dirt-piles at the regulation distance from the curbstone	1	2	3	D
46.	Failure to sweep properly	1	2	3	D
47.	Failure to take proper care of department property	2	3	5	D
48.	Absence from post of duty without reasonable excuse	2	3	5	D

Rule	CHARACTER OF OFFENSE	PENALTY Offense 1st	2d	3d	4th
49.	Failure to clean up any dirt, ashes, or garbage left or spilled upon the street or sidewalk by any department driver or drivers; or failure to report the facts to the foreman on same day, giving name or names and badge number or numbers of the driver or drivers, if known, with the exact place and time, as near as possible, at which such ashes or garbage was spilled or left upon the street or sidewalk	1	3	5	D
50.	Failure to replace receptacles within the stoop or area line after emptying the contents of same into cart	1	3	5	D

During the first year of my administration as commissioner of street-cleaning I found that in the maintenance of discipline frequent appeals from my decisions were made by the men. These decisions were necessarily based mainly on official reports. In order that no employee should be treated unjustly, I undertook, in the beginning, either to give each complainant a hearing myself, or to deputize some other official to do so for me. This occupied so much time as to interfere with the regular department business, and was not always satisfactory to the men themselves.

After a study of the Belgian method of "arbitration and conciliation," and of the experiences in this country of the mason builders and the bricklayers, I conceived a scheme which would afford the men an ample hearing before a competent and unprejudiced committee of their own creation. The earlier stages of each investigation would be absolutely under the control of this committee, and the entire force would be in close touch with its work.

The feature of this scheme which requires a preliminary consideration of all questions, whether personal or general, by a body constituted entirely of representatives of the employees themselves, is, I believe, original.

Early in January, 1896, I addressed the following

unofficial communication to the "Employees of the Department":

In order to establish friendly and useful relations between the men in the working-force and the officers of the department, I shall be glad to see an organization formed among the men for the discussion of all matters of interest.

This organization will be represented by five spokesmen in a "board of conference," in which the commissioner will be represented by the general superintendent, the chief clerk, one district superintendent, one section foreman, and one stable foreman.

It is suggested that the men who gather at each section station and the men at each stable (with the boardmen from the nearest dumps) each elect one of their number to represent them in a general committee of forty-one (thirty-two from section stations and nine from stables), and that this general committee elect the five spokesmen by whom it is to be represented in the Board of Conference.

The general committee will meet in a room, to be provided for it, at 2 P. M. on every Thursday, except the third Thursday of each month. The members will not have their time docked for this. Their meetings will be secret, and they will be expected to discuss with perfect freedom everything connected with their work, their relations with the commissioner and his subordinates, and all questions of discipline, duties, pay, etc., in which they are interested, or which their sections, stables, and dumps may have submitted to them.

The Board of Conference will meet at 2 P. M. on the third Thursday of each month, or as near to this date as the exigencies of the work will allow.

The ten members of the Board of Conference will be on a perfect equality. It will establish its own organization and rules of procedure, and will elect one of its members permanent chairman and another permanent secretary, one of these to be chosen from the five officers, and another from the five spokesmen.

It is hoped that this board will be able to settle every question that may come up to the satisfaction of all concerned, because most differences can be adjusted by discussions in which both sides are fairly represented.

Should any matter arise as to which the board cannot come to a substantial agreement, the permanent chairman and the permanent secretary will argue the case before the commissioner, who will try to reach a fair conclusion upon it.

In conformity with the foregoing call, the sweepers and drivers organized the Committee of Forty-one, representatives being chosen entirely by themselves. This committee, after several meetings, elected from its number five men—three sweepers and two drivers—to represent it in the Board of Conference.

The Board of Conference held its first meeting February 20, 1896. Every appointee was present, and in organizing the board a sweeper was unanimously chosen as permanent chairman, and the chief clerk as permanent secretary.

The following is taken from an account of the operations of the system, written by the secretary of the Board of Conference:

"From the beginning it was evident that a large number of the men had a very full appreciation of the purpose of the plan. They welcomed it in a manly spirit, and entered heartily into every detail of organization. This was the more strange in view of the radical change of venue, as it were. A large percentage of the men were members of, and amenable to, organizations which had existed in the department under former administrations, and the influence from these sources could not be expected to cease without an effort on the part of those whose success depended upon dissensions which might occur, or which they could create, between the commissioner and the men, and who often deceived and misled into serious and embarrassing situations those whose interests they were supposed to have at heart and to protect.

"Aside from those identified by membership with these organizations, there were many, not members, who held a latent sympathy with the old system of settling difficulties by strikes. In fact, it was generally understood that wrongs must be either borne or righted by coercion. Arbitration was looked upon as a far-off theory, applicable, perhaps, at times, somewhere, and under certain conditions; but the idea of its adaptation to and adoption by a municipal department of the city of New York, and especially by the Department of Street-Cleaning, where political preference was the only rule they had ever known, had never entered their minds. In fact, they were warned by skeptics, both outside of the department and among themselves, to 'look out for Waring; this is one of his tricks.' That any commissioner of street-cleaning, even though he were an 'angel,' should honestly intend and honestly endeavor to deal fairly with the rank and file of those under him was too much to believe. There must, they thought, be some sinister motive behind it.

"Gradually, however, the better element among the men did believe in it; and as their faith grew stronger the malcontents were either converted or thrust out, and slowly but surely the Committee of Forty-one became a body of earnest and honest coöperators with the commissioner toward the mutual confidence so essential for contentment on the part of the men, and without which the best results from the combined efforts of the commissioner and themselves could not be expected.

"A very false impression obtains among the public at large that the men constituting the membership of the department sweepers and drivers are below the average in intelligence and acumen. This is not the case. Not all of them have enjoyed the advantages of a scholarly education (although some of them have), but it would be a happy day for this country were the average legislator to display the fairness and judgment of these men who have been chosen by their respective constituents as representatives.

"Of course, in the beginning, and while the proposed plan of arbitration was an unknown quantity to the men, and they themselves unknown to each other, dead-wood drifted in and disturbing spirits appeared; but, as intimated above, this element was soon detected and in an orderly manner eliminated.

"The Committee of Forty-one has, since its first meeting, met every Thursday, except the third Thursday in each month. Its meetings are held with closed doors, and its discussions have, therefore, been free from any surveillance or influence, and, as was intended, entirely private and unrestrained.

"Perhaps the best way of explaining the general character of the work is to cite illustrating sample cases. For instance:

"Driver A of Stable —— has been reported by an inspector as entering a liquor saloon during working-hours and in full uniform, and remaining inside for ten minutes —this in violation of a very important rule, the penalty for the second offense being dismissal. Driver A admits entering the door of the saloon, and also admits remaining inside for ten minutes, but has an explanation to make as to his reasons for so doing. Argument in all such cases cannot be allowed, lest the officers of the department would have time for little else than to listen to lame excuses and bogus explanations. Driver A has now, however, another recourse. He calls upon his representative in the Committee of Forty-one and explains the matter to him fully, confirming his statement in writing. His representative submits the case at the next meeting of the committee, and there the plea of A is read and discussed by his co-laborers. His explanation is that the door which he entered is one of two leading to the saloon, but which also leads to a tenement in the rear of the saloon, in which he has his home. It appeared from his explanation that his wife had been confined recently, and that, as his home was on his way to the dump, his natural anxiety prompted him to stop for a moment. He submitted, in confirmation of his statement, the certificate of a reliable physician in the neighborhood, in whose hands his wife's case was, and, having requested his foreman to accompany him to his home, submitted a letter from him substantiating his statement. He also produced letters from both his foreman and his district superintendent stating that he was never known to have been under the influence of liquor, nor had he ever been charged with entering a saloon before. These officials said that he was a reliable and careful driver.

"At its next meeting the committee investigated the matter, and after gathering confirmatory testimony is persuaded that A's claim is a just one, and therefore referred the case to the Board of Conference, with such additional light as it had been able to obtain. This board is so constituted that no matter what the character of the case referred to it by the Committee of Forty-one may be, there is always one member representing the commissioner qualified by his position and experience to judge of its merits.

"The man has now taken his case two steps toward the commissioner, and thus far without the latter's knowledge. To facilitate quick adjustment, these matters are, before being considered by the board, referred in an informal way to one of its official members. This official brings with him to the meeting the result of his informal investigation and copies of the department records relating to the case. Thus the board is able to consider A's claim impartially, and also to determine its truthfulness. After due consideration the matter is referred to an official in the department having charge of such business, with the recommendation that the fine be remitted.

"By the foregoing process a budget of papers relating to each case is arranged in chronological order and submitted to the commissioner, who at a glance can comprehend it from beginning to end and quickly decide as to its merits. A report of his decision is added to the budget, and transmitted by the secretary of the Board of Conference to the secretary of the Committee of Forty-one, and it, among others, is read to the committee at its next meeting. In the case in question, where the commissioner's decision was in favor of the man, the amount forfeited by A was credited to him on the next pay-roll.

"The following case is somewhat different in character:

"At one of the board meetings a communication was received from the Committee of Forty-one calling attention to an ordinance of the city requiring householders to clear snow from the gutters in front of their premises, and pointing out the very great saving in expense to the city which would result were the ordinance enforced. Not only would it be a saving to the city, but it would afford quick relief to the public at cross-walks, which would otherwise be flooded in wet or thawing weather if there were snow on the ground. This matter was carefully considered by the board, and referred direct to the commissioner, with the suggestion that he request the assistance of the Police Department. The commissioner thanked the committee for its suggestion, and immediately took the matter up anew, having already conferred with the Police Department on the subject.

"It might appear at first glance that the machinery, as indicated above, is cumbersome and the process slow. Such, however, is not the case. The system is so precisely arranged that when once a case has been started it goes along without delay. No case need remain unsettled for more than thirty days after its submission to a representative or to the Committee of Forty-one direct, and, as a matter of fact, very many cases are settled by the Committee of Forty-one in half that time, or less.

"The matters referred by the committee to the Board of Conference vary in character. They are not all complaints. The board frequently receives suggestions from the men as to improvements in the department service, or perhaps for some modification or change of a rule. A number of these suggestions have been approved and adopted, and the service has been benefited thereby. Of course there are many cases submitted to the Committee of Forty-one which are so trivial that they are thrown out of court at once, and never reach even the Board of Conference. Occasionally, however, a complaint of this character does get through, perhaps inadvertently, and reaches the board; but it ends its career there.

"Of all the cases considered by the Board of Conference during its first year, there was but one upon which it could not agree. On this case the board was divided evenly, the representatives of the men on one side, and those of the commissioner on the other. This liability to a dead-lock had been anticipated in the original call, and provided for; accordingly, the chairman and the secretary of the board argued their respective sides of the question before the commissioner. This case, occurring toward the end of the year, was a novelty; and as the members of the board were very earnest in their respective convictions, the matter was watched with much interest, it being considered, as it were, a test case.

"The commissioner's decision in the matter was in favor of the complainant, and the fine which had been imposed was remitted. He stated, however, that 'technically, and in accordance with all rules of discipline, the fine was a just one, and should be imposed in all similar cases. At the same time, I cannot avoid the feeling that this violation was made for no improper reason, and perhaps with a laudable desire to help the service; and, in any case, probably the ends of justice and discipline are as fully satisfied by the mental anxiety to which the driver has been subjected, and the full discussion the subject has received in the Committee of Forty-one and the Board of Conference, as they would be by the enforcement of the penalty. I therefore direct that the fine be remitted.'"

The following is a brief statistical statement of the year's work of the Board of Conference, and relates entirely to cases referred to it by the Committee of Forty-one, or matters brought up by the members of the board representing the men:

Matters explained satisfactorily at the same meeting at which submitted	15
Fines remitted or reduced	22

Fines sustained 13
Suggestions from employees for the comfort and convenience of the men, or for the betterment of the department service, approved and acted upon by the commissioner 24
Cases considered by the board, but on which it determined that no action should be taken 14
Employees dismissed, reinstated upon satisfactory evidence that the dismissals were unmerited 8
Employees dismissed, but, because of unsatisfactory explanations, not reinstated 17
The total number of cases considered by the board (an average of over ten for each meeting) 124

The above is in no way connected with the statistics of cases considered or matters discussed at the meetings of the Committee of Forty-one.

During the year the Committee of Forty-one considered 345 cases, of which 124 were referred to the Board of Conference, 221 being settled satisfactorily by itself.

So far as I have been permitted to judge, the system of arbitration as above outlined has appealed to the men as a straightforward and perfectly open channel for the communication of their grievances, and the officers of the department who are in closest relations with the employees so describe the generally prevailing feeling. In the beginning, however, as has been said already, this feeling was tinctured with a quite natural suspicion that the scheme was a cut-and-dried affair, and that the delegates elected would be so subservient to official influences that their consideration of the various cases coming before them would, under the flattery of implied power, be merely perfunctory. In other words, it was regarded as a sop to stay the growth of that repressed bitterness under injustice and injury—real or fancied—which, in the old days, had so often culminated in an outbreak that was the only method known to the men of asserting themselves, and whose power for causing harm and suffering to the people of the entire city they so well appreciated.

Except from an occasional malcontent, whose dismissal is the consequence of some offense so flagrant and apparent that his case receives but scant consideration in the Committee of Forty-one, we no longer hear that the delegates are the commissioner's men, and not the laborers' representatives. Indeed, the men themselves realize that the preponderance of leaning, so far, has been toward their side, the five officers representing the commissioner in the Board of Conference, in their desire to be perfectly fair and to avoid even the appearance of arbitrariness, preferring to exercise too much leniency rather than too little.

The Committee of Forty-one corresponds in one way to any other representative body; but it is a great deal more. Each one of its members is elected by a small circle of men to every one of whom he is intimately known through the association of daily labor performed in common. This man must jealously watch and guard the interests of his constituents, or be obliged by them to give place to one who will do so. But the most marked difference of all lies in the fact that the delegate is forced to present the complaint of any one of his constituents to the Committee of Forty-one. He has no chance for the display of favoritism, nor can he be the recipient of bribes from individuals or lobbies. There is always a hearing for any constituent, however weak or preposterous his plea. Should he, however, be refused by his delegate, or should his case be neglected, he may go directly before a member of the Board of Conference and receive a sanction for the consideration of his complaint by the Committee of Forty-one. Furthermore, the session of the Committee of Forty-one is never adjourned *sine die*, and no case can be crowded out or rushed through for lack of time.

As will readily be seen, a delegate in his daily associations is under constant surveillance by his constituents. All of his working hours are office hours for his fellows, and he can escape their importunities only by resignation. Some of the men who have found the position the reverse of the honorable sinecure they were seeking have given way to others who are prepared to assume, at a considerable sacrifice and with unselfish zeal, the extra work and the great responsibility entailed. It is only fair to the laboring-man to say that among no other class is this disinterested devotion to the welfare of his mates more frequently met with.

The presence of a delegate in each of the divisions of the laboring-body is, in its way, a check upon the conduct of the foremen. Discipline, which is the life of the department, is in no manner interfered with. On the contrary, it is effectually freed of the objections so often resulting from the excessive use of authority. Harshness, loud-mouthed profanity, and brutality are not likely to be indulged in by foremen, with so powerful an intermediary as the delegate always present. Naturally he is not allowed to interfere actively. During his working-hours he is a laborer pure and simple, and superiors must be obeyed, no matter how unjust or unreasonable they may be. His power begins only with his weekly appearance as a member in the Committee of Forty-one, where, alone with his fellows, he is given the opportunity of stating his case with any degree of heat that may seem to him fitting, and with the certainty that it will be judged by no one but laborers with similar associations and like sympathies. The committee transmits it, divested of all incidents of passion, to the Board of Conference, where the laborer is, for the nonce, on an absolute equality with his officer.

Thus far our arbitration system has proved a most gratifying success, and it is with much pleasure that I note its indorsement by practical business men and large factory-owners. It has, I am firmly convinced, a bright and growing future, not only as far as this department is concerned, but in the general adjustment of the labor question throughout the country.

I indulge the hope that the modest experiment here described may prove, in its expansion, to be a factor of no inconsiderable importance in the ultimate solution of vexed questions of difference between employer and employed. Even if it be shown to be limited in sphere to its present field of action, its creation has certainly not been in vain. The benefit it has conferred on this department by suppressing the tendency to strike, by the creation of an *esprit de corps*, and by cementing men and officers together in a bond of common sympathy and fellow-feeling, has been of incalculable assistance toward the results I have striven to achieve. It has not only furnished a channel for settling individual grievances, but it has prevented misunderstandings between the men and their commissioner, and has given him the means for ascertaining their real feelings in regard to changes in policy, new rules, methods, and equipment. In a word, with but little labor and the slightest tax upon his time, it has brought him face to face with every one of his three thousand employees.

CHAPTER V

STREET-SWEEPING

NATURALLY the most obvious, as well as the most important, part of the work of street-cleaning is that which is done in removing accumulations from the surface of the streets. In New York forty per cent. of the entire disbursement of the department is for sweeping, and sixty per cent. of the laboring-force is employed in this part of the work, which here is done entirely by hand.

Machine-sweeping was formerly almost universal, especially when work was done by contract; and, as a rule, contract street-cleaning throughout the country is executed in this way. At the beginning of operations under the present administration there was still a considerable amount of work done by machines, which were employed almost universally at night. The dust raised by them, even with preliminary sprinkling, constituted such a nuisance as to make it improper to sweep by machine during the day. After very careful comparisons of cost and of the character of the work done, it was determined that there was little, if any, economy in using machines if they were made to do the best work of which they are capable, and that it was not possible, under any circumstances, to do such uniformly good work by machinery as by hand. In the summer of 1895 the use of machines was entirely abandoned. Two years' experience with hand-work has satisfied me that it is incomparably more advantageous than machine-work, and it is not likely that the latter will again be resorted to in this city.

We have four hundred and thirty-three miles of paved streets (which alone receive our attention); and we have actually at work, at this writing, about fourteen hundred and fifty sweepers—broom-men. This gives a little less than one third of a mile, on an average, to each sweeper. There are naturally great deviations in this respect, the actual number used in different parts of the city varying about from one to a mile to seven to a mile, according to the character of the pavement, the character and density of the population, the character of the district, whether manufacturing, resident, tenement, etc., and the character and amount of traffic. It is to be understood that under the law our men work only eight hours per day. This short time is to an important degree offset by the fact that their places are very desirable, and that they work hard, and in emergencies for longer hours, in order that they may keep their places. It is a further inducement that their positions are permanent. Under the law as it now exists, and is likely to remain, an employee of the department can only be dismissed for cause. One of these causes is incapacity, so that these are by no means life-positions, but good only for the effective working-years of life.

That part of Manhattan Island lying below One Hundred and Fifty-second Street is divided into fifty-eight sections, having pretty uniformly seven miles of street each. The number of men in these sections varies from fifteen to thirty-five. Each section is under the control of a foreman, who has one or two assistants. The uniform of the foreman consists of a close-fitting grayish-brown coat, buttoned to the throat, with a rolling collar; trousers of the same; a white helmet; and a shield similar to the police badge. The assistants wear the same uniform, with a small silver-plated delta (Δ) hanging below the shield. The sweepers are dressed entirely in white duck. The coat is a sort of

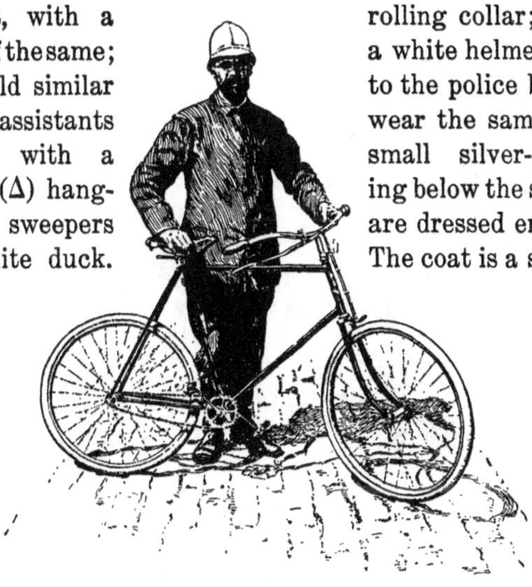

A SECTION FOREMAN.

Norfolk jacket, with a leather belt and metal clasp, with metal buttons; trousers which are rather loose; and they wear helmets similar to those of the foremen. Each wears on his left breast an oval metal badge bearing his number. He is obliged to appear always at morning roll-call in a tidy condition. As a rule, the suits are changed on Thursday and on Monday, but if soiled from any cause they must be changed more frequently. Each suit costs one dollar and twenty-five cents. The cost of the entire outfit—two suits, five buttons, belt and clasp, and helmet with monogram—is four dollars and sixty-three cents.

Each sweeper is supplied with the following implements: a two-wheeled bag-carrier and a sufficient number of jute bags for his day's work; a broom of African bass with a steel scraper at its back, a shovel,

A SWEEPER WITH HIS BAG-CARRIER AND TOOLS.

and a short broom. In summer he carries also a watering-can and a key for opening hydrants. If he has any considerable amount of asphalt in his beat, he uses for this a steel scraper about three feet broad, which is very effective for taking up fresh droppings and other accumulations.

If the section is traversed by one or more avenues of heavy traffic, a number—and sometimes all—of the men of the section are worked in gangs early in the morning for the first thorough cleaning of these. After that they disperse and go each to his own route. As a rule, this route is not changed; the same sweeper is employed upon it from one end of the year to the other. He becomes familiar with its people, its shops, its stables, and whatever else may have to do with the incidents of his work. Occasionally, from some change of condition, the amount of work to be done is permanently increased. In such cases the length of the route may be shortened; but ordinarily, if a man grows slack in his methods and fails to keep the route in good order, he is dismissed and a more capable man put in his place.

SWEEPER'S TOOLS.

The sprinkler must be used always in dry weather, during the season when it is allowed to open the hydrants—from April to November. Fines are imposed for raising a dust. The accumulations on the streets, of whatever character, are, where necessary, loosened by the scraper, and are then swept into little piles within a short radius. These are then, with the aid of the broom and shovel, transferred to the bag, which is held open by the carrier. When the bag is filled it is stood on the edge of the sidewalk. In wet weather, when the sweepings are in a state of solution, they are allowed to stand in piles until the free water has drained away; but even then the material is wet and heavy, the bags are much less easy to handle, and the cart-horses are apt to be overloaded because of this.

A few remote streets of little population and light traffic are kept in suitable condition with one daily sweeping; ordinary streets are swept twice a day, and others from three to five times, according to the exigencies of the case.

At present the work is divided about as follows:

63½	miles	are	swept	once a day;
283½	"	"	"	twice a day;
50½	"	"	"	three times a day;
35½	"	"	"	four or more times a day.

This makes a total average sweeping of 924. This is not perfunctory work. The streets are really clean, and except for the littering, which the police have not yet succeeded in preventing, they always look clean. Mud is unknown, and dust is vastly diminished in comparison with former conditions.

CHAPTER VI

CARTING

NEXT in importance to the sweeping of the streets is the work of removing not only the product of the sweeping, but all domestic and some trade wastes, such as ashes, garbage, paper, and rubbish. In the New York department thirty-two per cent. of the disbursement is for "carting," and twenty-five per cent. of the laboring-force is employed in this part of the work. This includes about six hundred drivers, with horses and carts. Most of the stable force is charged to carting.

The carts start out from the various stables at an early hour, and go to the sections to which they are assigned, the same men generally working on the same routes year in and year out. They first remove a load of ashes. After this they devote themselves to the carting of garbage until this is all removed. The rest of the day is occupied in collecting the remaining ashes and the sweepings that may have been gathered during the day. As the sweeping continues until four o'clock, the cartmen are obliged to work much later. They take from one and a half to two hours' "swing" at noon, but even so they work regularly more than the eight hours required of the sweepers. We try to so arrange it that every cart shall return to the stable before 6 P. M., but even this is not always possible.

In the down-town district, owing to the crowded condition of the streets during the day, it is necessary that both sweeping and carting be done at night. There is very little population here, and the material to be removed is mainly incident to business traffic.

The garbage hauls are very long, as there are only six garbage-dumps for the whole city. These dumps are supplied with scows or other vessels by the Utilization Company. The department loads the garbage upon these vessels, and its connection with this portion of the work is then at an end. For street-sweepings and ashes we have seventeen dumps at different points, so located as to be within convenient reach, except in the case of the district lying west of Central Park. On that side of the city we have no dumping facilities of any kind between Forty-seventh Street and One Hundred and Thirty-first Street, a distance of nearly five miles. The removal from the central portion of this district is across the park to the foot of Eightieth Street, East River—a distance of two and a half miles, but over very much better grades than the route to Forty-seventh Street or to One Hundred and Thirty-first Street.

The street-sweepings are collected in bags, as described in the previous chapter. The bags are loaded on the carts without being untied, and are emptied at the dump, where they are cleaned and dried for the next day's use.

Thus far ashes are almost entirely collected from metal cans and other receptacles which are set on the sidewalk inside of the stoop-line or in the areas in front of the houses. It is in contemplation soon to extend throughout the city an improved system which has been in successful operation for more than a year. Under this system, each house is supplied with a can supported on a tripod six or eight inches above the floor. It has a hinged cover, and the bottom is closed by two flap-doors. The cartman takes a bag into the house or area or back yard,—for it is only required that the can be kept out of sight of the street and protected from the rain,—passes the bag under and around the can, and attaches it to the top frame of the tripod. He then closes the cover to prevent the flying of dust, and operates the mechanism which opens the doors at the bottom. The ashes run out into the bag, which is tied and set on the sidewalk to be removed with the sweepings. These bags also are emptied only at the dump.

Formerly the practice prevailed of removing in the same cart the sweepings shoveled from little piles in the streets and the entire waste of the house, which was put indiscriminately into the receptacles—garbage, ashes, paper, rubbish, and everything, save only such large objects as furniture, mattresses, etc. In 1896 the separation of these materials was taken in hand, and has now been completely effected.

The treatment of all other material than garbage, sweepings, and ashes remains to be described. The removal of this constitutes what we call the "paper and rubbish" service. It is ordered that all wastes of this class be kept in the house, or at least under cover and out of sight of the street. A cart of special construction is used for the removal of this material. It is a very large low-hung box on two wheels, and is drawn by a lighter and more active horse than is required for the heavy loads of the sweepings and ash service. This material is called for only on the exposure—as in the basement window—of a special "call" card. This is red and of diamond shape, with the letters "P. R." in conspicuous form in white on the front. Printed instructions are given on the reverse side.

This card relates to the following articles: paper, general rubbish, bottles, rags, tin cans, excelsior, pasteboard boxes, old shoes, leather and rubber scrap, carpets, broken glass, barrels, boxes, discarded furniture, wood, and all metals.

Thus far the carts carrying these wastes dump their loads upon the scows which also receive the sweepings and ashes, but measures are now being taken to deliver them at "Picking-yards," where a thorough sorting will be done and everything of salable value culled out and made ready for the market. This is more fully described in Chapter X.

CHAPTER VII

FINAL DISPOSITION OF GARBAGE

A TIME-HONORED custom of the city of New York has been to send its garbage to sea with all of its other wastes, save only the fat and bones collected by the scow-trimming Italians at the dumps. By far the largest proportion of garbage consists of vegetable refuse, much of which floats in sea-water. As a result of this method of disposal, the bathing beaches of New Jersey and Long Island have often been made unfit for use by the immense amount of offensive material washed ashore, especially during storms, and the water in the front of the beaches is often too foul for bathing because of the watermelon-rinds, cabbage-leaves, etc., floating in it.

The outcry for years against this fouling of the beaches has been loud and strenuous. Efforts have been made on the part of the authorities of the State of New York and of the United States to seek a practicable remedy. This remedy has at last been found in the separation of garbage from all other material, and its delivery to a company which is charged with its care. My expert assistants have been actively engaged in the consideration of this subject since the very beginning of this administration. The result of their investigations is well set forth in the following report of Mr. Macdonough Craven, in chief charge of the investigation, written in December, 1895, as follows:

REPORT OF MACDONOUGH CRAVEN ON THE PRELIMINARY INVESTIGATIONS MADE FOR THE DEPARTMENT AS TO GARBAGE AND ITS TREATMENT

When it was decided, early in the year, to dispose of the city's garbage by some better method than the old process of dumping at sea, an effort was made to learn what system would be best suited to the city of New York, with its limited space and its large amount of material to be cared for daily, and what the economies of such a system might be.

Early in March last, therefore, the various companies in this country engaged in the treatment of garbage were invited to present to this department informal bids showing the prices at which they would be willing to receive and properly dispose of the garbage of New York City.

Twenty-six answers were received and opened on March 26, but only one company was willing to accept a contract from the city without a subsidy to aid in the work. The average of all bids from companies which proposed to cremate or destroy by fire was ninety cents per ton of garbage delivered, to be paid by the city; and from companies which proposed to utilize the garbage, or convert its available parts into grease and fertilizer, the average of all bids was fifty-five cents per ton. Only about half of the twenty-six bidders were believed by the department to be sufficiently experienced and responsible to make offers from them acceptable to the city.

Under these circumstances, it was deemed advisable to make an independent investigation of the various methods proposed, since, on the one hand, the city should not be allowed to pay more than, under economical management, would secure efficient service, while, on the other hand, it would be disastrous to accept a low bid from any company which, on limited experience, might have underestimated the cost, and find itself losing money and obliged to cease operations. No financial return in the form of bonded security could recompense the city if it should find its garbage uncared for in the midst of a heated summer.

Acting upon this theory, a circular letter was prepared and sent to each of the companies, proposing an examination of its plant and system by two competent men from this department, the scope of the examination to include the cost of operation, the value of the commercial products, and the very important questions of the permissible character of the process and its adaptability to the needs of this city; the minimum time of test to be thirty days; the salaries and expenses of the examiners to be paid by the company; the numerical results of the test to be considered confidential information to this department.

Several of the companies acquiesced in the value of such an examination, and expressed their willingness to accede to its terms.

Competent men were therefore selected for the work, different ones being sent to different plants, in order that the examination might be impartial and unprejudiced, and the result obtained within a reasonably short time. The tests were of necessity summer tests, when garbage becomes most quickly offensive, when any odors arising from the treatment would surely be noticeable, and when also garbage contains most water and is least valuable for utilization purposes.

More than three thousand tons of garbage in the cities of Buffalo, St. Louis, Philadelphia, Brooklyn, and New York were treated by different methods, under the supervision of your inspectors.

One point made clear by the investigation is that when garbage is collected daily from each house, from clean cans, and conveyed at once to a properly equipped reduction plant, it has not time to ferment, even in summer, before it is safely stowed away within the steam-tight cooking-tanks of the reduction plant; and that under these conditions, and under experienced management, the operations of such a factory can be carried on with little more offense than arises from a large kitchen.

The first difficulty experienced, in the endeavor to operate a satisfactory system of collection and disposal, arises from the tendency of some householders to consider the cleanliness of the private garbage-can as the affair of the city. If the householder daily delivers to the garbage-collector only the table and kitchen refuse of the past twenty-four hours, it is evident that there cannot be serious offense in what was so lately fit for the table; but if the can is not thoroughly cleaned each day after being emptied, it will soon give rise to odors and just complaints.

The second difficulty is found in the natural tendency of men engaged in handling such waste material to regard it as essentially unclean, and therefore to fail to maintain in a state of cleanliness the carts, wagons, and machinery in use.

When our observations on this point are condensed, they amount simply to a statement of the facts that garbage twenty-four hours old is not offensive to the smell, either in small or in large quantities, but that even minute remnants do become offensive in two or three days, and that only unremitting care can keep the cans, carts, and machinery employed in a cleanly condition.

Kitchen refuse consists of animal and vegetable scrap, containing and mixed with a large amount of water. The animal scrap is of value for utilization purposes, because it furnishes the principal part of the grease and ammonia which are the salable products of garbage; and since the cost of treating such waste is approximately the same, be it rich or poor, it is plain that the commercial value of garbage varies almost directly as its proportion of animal matter. If the amount of grease and ammonia recovered are sufficient to defray the expense of treatment, the people of any city may have their garbage disposed of without cost; and while this condition probably does not now exist anywhere on the continent, it is an end worth striving for if it can be accomplished without loss to the householder.

Some practices of the citizen which affect the value of garbage have been reported. A large proportion of people keep uncovered garbage-cans or -barrels, and a vast majority of these keep them in yards or outhouses, where they are accessible to every stray cat or prowling dog that comes, and soon they come regularly. Some of the investigators have watched troops of cats making their nightly rounds from yard to yard, pulling out of each accustomed barrel and can the accessible pieces of meat, bone, and other delicacies; and thus not only is a public nuisance maintained in the form of a howling mob of homeless cats, but the garbage is culled of the only parts that go to make it valuable to a contractor or help to reduce the price which the city must pay for its disposal.

The same trouble intensified is found when garbage is collected only three times, or perhaps twice, a week. The cats and dogs do just so much more work. And then, too, the tidy housekeeper, to whom a waste-can is an eyesore under the best of circumstances, gets tired of smelling or imagining the odors due to two or three days' decomposition, and begins to consign, not to the garbage-can, but to the kitchen fire, all that burns most easily—of course the scraps containing grease. This is waste of good material, but it is much better than foul odors and the midnight cat. If in this city, where garbage is collected daily, the householder will only keep a cover on his can, he will do much toward lessening the cost of final disposition.

One can scarcely conceive of a crematory which destroys garbage by fire becoming a self-supporting concern, since considerable fuel is necessary and the only residue is ashes; but the fact that there are garbage "utilization" plants at once suggests that under certain conditions the utilizable material may pay for its own extraction. It is perhaps needless to say that the word "garbage"—which is so loosely used in this and a few other cities to denote any kind of waste, or a mixture of them all, including ashes and street-sweepings—is for the purpose of this investigation limited to animal and vegetable refuse from markets and kitchens. Only this is desirable in a utilization plant. A small admixture of cans, bottles, and berry-boxes entails extra expense for separation, but is not prohibitory of the process, while any such mixture as we have in New York to-day, of ashes, garbage, and a little of everything, *is* prohibitory. Garbage must be separated from everything else to be effectively and properly treated, and the other things must be separated from garbage to find, in their turn, any useful outlet.

In connection with the tests, I beg to call attention to the uniform courtesy with which the examiners have been received, and the willing assistance offered at the various working plants inspected. As noted above, the salaries and all expenses of the examiners, and the additional costs incidental to the tests, have been cheerfully borne by the companies, and no trouble or expense has been spared by them to further the interests of the investigation. The Merz Universal Extractor and Construction Company submitted its operations to our inspection for a term of four weeks in Buffalo and two in St. Louis; and for a further test of New York and Brooklyn garbage, and to demonstrate the Preston process, which is controlled by the above company, experiments were carried on for two weeks in a special plant in Greenpoint, Long Island. The Sanative Refuse Company, at an expense of several thousand dollars, equipped a plant in New York City and conducted a continuous test of two months for the purpose of allowing us to study their system and to learn the character and composition of New York garbage. The works of the American Incinerating Company in Philadelphia treated eighteen hundred tons to illustrate their utilization system and the character of Philadelphia garbage, while, for a similar purpose in Brooklyn, the American Reduction Company reduced eighty-four tons under our inspection. The Holthaus plant at Bridgeport, Connecticut, has undergone an exhaustive and costly test; and as the company operating this system apparently does not receive all the garbage of the city, it is working under difficulties and at an unnecessary expense. Notwithstanding this, however, every facility has been given to the department examiners.

The Standard Construction and Utilization Company of Philadelphia was inspected under the same conditions as the above-named companies, but, owing to difficulties unforeseen by its managers, it proved impossible to complete the test.

Systematically arranged, the tests already made appear as follows:

NAME OF COMPANY	LOCATION	DATE
Merz Universal Extractor and Construction Company	Buffalo . .	June
Merz Universal Extractor and Construction Company	St. Louis .	July
Sanative Refuse Company . . .	New York .	August

At these three plants grease is extracted by the use of hydrocarbon oils, and the remaining solids are converted into a fertilizer base.

NAME OF COMPANY	LOCATION	DATE
The Preston process	Greenpoint .	July
The Bridgeport Utilization Company . .	Bridgeport .	February
American Incinerating Company . .	Philadelphia	July

At these three plants grease is extracted by mechanical pressure, and the remaining solids are made into a fertilizer base.

NAME OF COMPANY	LOCATION	DATE
Sanative Refuse Company (Pierce process)	New York .	September
American Reduction Company . .	Brooklyn .	May

Both these companies make the garbage solids into a complete fertilizer ready for the farmer's use, but the first extracts the grease by means of a solvent, while the second uses acid.

NAME OF COMPANY	LOCATION	DATE
The Standard Construction and Utilization Company	Philadelphia	August

At this plant the cooking is done in steam-jacketed caldrons, the charge being agitated meanwhile, and the grease separated by flotation and skimming.

These comprise most of the best-known systems, and illustrate nearly all of what in this country has been reduced to practice in the treatment of garbage. As yet we have derived from the house and hotel garbage only grease and fertilizer materials. Our two best-known means of extracting the grease are (1) by dissolving it in some liquid which, after being drawn off, may be separated from the grease and recovered, and (2) the mechanical method of forcing out warm grease under heavy pressure. During this summer's tests these two methods, and all others submitted, were carefully examined as to the cost of operation and the results obtained. The importance of this becomes at once evident when it is known that the forty to fifty pounds of grease in a ton of garbage may be extracted in such condition as to sell for three and a half cents per pound, making in value about half the available material in garbage, and that if any remains unextracted it is doubly lost, since it detracts from the selling value of the fertilizer.

The facts to be learned, then, in reference to grease extraction by each method were (1) the cost of operation; (2) the amount of grease extracted; (3) its condition—freedom from dirt, water, etc.; (4) the amount unextracted; and by determining these four points we have not only established the relative efficiencies of the different methods practised, but have learned the character and value of New York garbage as compared with that of other cities.

A special paper upon the condition and probable future of the grease trade has been prepared from information furnished by dealers and consumers expert in the business, and this enables us to give to garbage grease, offered in small or in large quantities, its proper place and value, and to gage the accuracy of estimates which determine the figures submitted by bidders.

Regarding the solid matter of garbage, which after being

cooked becomes tankage or fertilizer base or complete fertilizer, there has been established a similar kind of information as to (1) the cost of getting rid of the water; (2) the amount of dry matter saved (and it is strange that the same kind of garbage shows such various results by different methods); (3) the condition of this dry matter—whether it is in a form suitable for the fertilizer manufacturer (and again it is strange how it varies); and (4) the amount of solid matter lost.

Here, too, a paper on the fertilizer trade, similar to that on the grease trade, has been prepared, and from similar sources.

The relation of these factories to the health of the community in which they are situated is determined by the cleanliness of the building and machinery, the manner and condition in which the garbage water is got rid of, and the character and amount of odors which escape. So much progress has been made of late years, and so many difficulties have been overcome, some by one company and some by another, that it seems safe now to say that if the best that is known on the subject could be put into practice in one factory, that factory could with freedom be located in any city on the continent.

It has been found necessary also to make a detailed study, covering several weeks, of the present disposition of the garbage and grease wastes of the city hotels, restaurants, and large boarding-houses. Many of these had made contracts with private parties for the disposal of their garbage before the city was in position to care for it, and even since that time the hours of removal by the city have not always met the necessities of such establishments, and many of the private contracts have been continued. This study was part of the general plan for determining the character and amount of recoverable kitchen waste in this city of meat-eaters not noted for excessive economy, and a valuable part, since in these places the separation of garbage from other matters has always been carefully made.

An examination of the libraries has furnished much useful information from the cities of Europe in reference to the amount of their garbage, its value, and the adopted methods of disposal, and both prepared the way for a comparison of their methods with ours, and enabled us to set a standard below which we need not fall.

The reports from the various examiners, upon being submitted, have been collated and corresponding tables prepared. A general report is herewith submitted.

The methods considered cover the hydrocarbon, acid, and mechanical processes.

Hydrocarbon processes extract the grease more thoroughly than any other method inspected.

Acid processes do not, as a rule, give good results as far as grease is concerned.

Mechanical processes extract a fair percentage of the grease.

The tankage is of varying quality, according to the method used and the class of garbage handled. All reduction methods, properly conducted, can be made unobjectionable from the sanitary point of view. The faults seem to come from a want of experience in construction, for what has been found offensive in one plant has been so handled in another as to be entirely without offense.

The material received in the different cities shows a great difference. This is due to the following causes:

1. Season of the year.
2. Geographical and trade location of the city.
3. Variation of the regulations in force.
4. Delinquencies of the officials in enforcing proper separation, and the consequent carelessness of the collectors, resulting in the delivery at the dumps or works of many things not properly belonging to city garbage.

The different seasons of the year show different classes of garbage. During the winter the garbage is less in bulk and greater in weight. This is due to the fact that many canned and only a few green vegetables are used. During the summer the quantity is larger, but the weight in proportion to the bulk is less. This is due to the fact that the green stuff or waste from fresh vegetables is predominant. During the summer months, also, a much larger proportion of refuse incidental to the handling of fruits and vegetables is mixed with the garbage. The different seasons may also be divided, as, for example, periods covering such as green-corn time, pea-pod time, melon time, and so on.

Geographical location controls garbage to the extent of determining the classes of vegetable and animal food that are in general use. Furthermore, as all cities are more or less trade centers and cosmopolitan in character, the floating population varies with the season of the year, and the markets' business varies in accordance therewith. The increase in population makes an increase in the waste.

The regulations of the various municipalities in some cases permit rubbish to be mixed with the garbage, and the quality and quantity of this rubbish are not clearly defined.

The delinquencies of officials, drivers, collectors, etc., arise from carelessness, personal gain by collusion with those interested in the works or with the householders, or an honest belief that they can improve on regulations and benefit the cities thereby. The last-mentioned class is very small.

It is found by investigation that the averages of collection and disposal vary. This variation can be traced to several causes:

1. Method of disposition.
2. Whether the city or a contractor makes the collections.
3. The regulations; that is, whether they permit of the garbage being overhauled by rag-pickers, etc.
4. Frequency of collections.

If the garbage and general refuse are hauled to dumps, and the haul is long, the cartmen or drivers, especially in rainy or otherwise disagreeable weather, if opportunity offers, will lessen their work by dumping at the most convenient place.

If the city refuse is burned, the material best adapted to the furnace is generally delivered, that is, combustible refuse.

If, on the other hand, it is reduced, combustible refuse is not especially desirable.

If the city makès the collections, and the cartmen are not closely supervised, they are liable to give poor service, and the householder, in order to improve on that service, will employ private collectors.

The collections made by private cartmen are not handled by the city as a rule, and therefore all record of such collections is lost.

Again, if a contractor makes the collections, it depends largely on the basis of payment; that is, if the payments are made in a lump sum, the tendency of the contractor is to collect as small a quantity as possible, whereas, if the payment is per ton or per cubic yard, there is a tendency to collect everything of sufficient weight or bulk to make the collection as large as possible. Percentages of collections *per capita*, therefore, vary.

The third case under consideration depends on the inspectors, police, health board, or whomsoever controls the work or supervises it. Should the supervision be lax, or the regulations permit, a large part of the refuse will be culled from the receptacles by rag-pickers and scavengers, and large quantities will thus be disposed of in an insalutary manner, also to the detriment of correct data of quantity, and the streets will be strewn with rubbish as well.

Nothing better than the method of collection pursued in this city has so far presented itself.

The frequency of collection has a strong bearing on the quantity collected. This is shown by the annexed tables, and may be due to several causes. Infrequent collection affords more opportunities for scavengers, both men and animals, to overhaul and deplete the waste.

The rubbish mixed with garbage is mainly tin cans; besides these there are bottles, rags, crockery, berry-baskets (especially in fruit season), wood scraps, metal, and all conceivable kinds of refuse. A three-foot section of sixty-pound T-rail was delivered at one of the works as garbage.

The cans are sold, the solder is in some cases recovered, and the body of the can melted down. They are a great nuisance to reduction plants, as in several processes they, or a part of them, are dumped into the extractors or the driers, as the case may be. If these cans do not fall bottom side up in the extractors, they not only hold what grease is in them, but also whatever finds its way into them while in the extractor. The cans in quantity in the driers cause considerable wear on the machinery, which may more than offset their value as auxiliary disintegrators, as will be set forth in the discussion on driers.

Those that are culled from the fresh or green garbage—all rubbish, in fact, culled from garbage—should be disinfected before being marketed.

The next matter of importance, as far as rubbish is concerned, is the rags. These rags are in some cases delivered with the garbage in large quantities. They are culled for various reasons—for marketing, to be used as combustibles in furnaces, and also to keep them clear of the machinery, which they are liable to clog to a great extent, more especially in rotary driers.

The other rubbish, with the exception of the bottles and crockery, is generally thrown into the furnace and consumed.

The above remarks apply more generally to reduction plants than to crematories, as in crematories combustible refuse mixed with the garbage aids and cheapens the cost of cremation, and tin cans keep the garbage more or less separated, thus permitting the heat to work through.

Nearly all the nuisances that arise or are complained of in regard to garbage originate from the free water mixed with the garbage. This drips from the carts, or is spilled from them in dumping, in varying quantities. It has that sour or swill smell so prevalent and so well known. This free water can be traced to three causes: rain, waste water of cooking, exudations from the vegetables themselves.

The rain-water is not, as a rule, of sufficient quantity to demand attention. If, however, the haul is long, the cart open, and the receptacles have been standing some time before collection, then the quantity of rain-water mixed with the garbage is more than would be expected, and is, in fact, at times very large. The usual quantity of free water is in the neighborhood of ten per cent. by weight, or from twenty-five to thirty gallons per ton.

The waste water of cooking forms a large part of the ten per cent.,—in fact, nearly all of it,—and is something to be avoided. Should it go to the sewer? Certainly it should not be permitted to pollute the public streets through the bottoms of leaky carts. The small quantity which exudes from the garbage itself can hardly be considered.

It is this swill water and the grease which clings to the sides and bottoms of the household receptacles and of the garbage carts which make them offensive; and if these receptacles and carts are not cleansed properly, and as often as necessary, the foul odors which arise give constant and just cause for complaint. This free water is not desired by crematories, but is advantageous to certain reduction plants.

In connection with the above, it might be well to speak of the receptacles and carts in general use.

The receptacles are not, as a rule, of the proper shape, being cylindrical in form and too high in proportion to the diameter, making them difficult to empty. A receptacle of wide mouth and narrow bottom could be more rapidly emptied, more easily cleansed, and would therefore be more acceptable to both the householder and the cartman.

"Galvanized-iron pails with covers are recommended. If the contents are kept properly dry, fermentation and the production of offensive gases are avoided, even although the temperature of the air is high" ("A Treatise on Hygiene and Public Health").

The carts in general use are of metal and tight-bottomed. The patterns vary; some are covered, some open.

"Large metal carts, like our 'trucks,' with springs to prevent noise, and with close-fitting wooden covers, made in sections, so that the entire cover need not be raised for the introduction of each pailful of garbage, are most in favor in German cities."

Daily removal is best.

After culling, the garbage treated at the different works

visited was, as a rule, similar in character. It was principally summer garbage and largely vegetable and fruit waste. This summer garbage, on account of its bulk, has to be handled more rapidly than that of the winter. It is therefore not so carefully culled, although, as it contains fewer ingredients of value, it may be more rapidly worked.

The winter garbage does not contain so much vegetable waste, but on account of the season of the year, and the large quantities of ice occasionally contained therein, more fuel is necessary to dispose of it; but the value of winter garbage is greater than that of summer.

The variation in the per cent. of useless tailings from reduction plants is due to the "efficiency of separation" by the cities, also to the manner of screening in use at the various works; but it is not due to the process. That is, the percentage of available solid matter for fertilizer contained in garbage is practically constant, but if the authorities permit extraneous matter to be mixed with the garbage, or if the mesh of the screen used in screening dried tankage is small, then the per cent. of waste is increased.

These tailings are used for various purposes, but are generally burned. They have a distinct value, as compared with coal, as a fuel. Although the fires have to be carefully cleansed after each burning of tailings, still they reduce the price of fuel per ton of garbage worked.

In many of the processes more of the tailings could be used for fertilizer if the process of separating them was complete. The only question is, Would a more expensive process, and one taking more time, pay for the slight additional percentage of available tankage over and above the gain made by the tailings used as fuel?

The gases and vapors that are driven off from the garbage during the working of the same are disposed of in two ways—by condensation and by cremation.

Vapors that are condensed are liable to be more offensive in the end than those that are burned. Condensation also is not liable to be very effective, as the foul vapors are driven off together with large quantities of steam. The steam and vapors will naturally mix as far as possible. These vapors, surcharged with steam, are carried to the condenser and there expected to take up or to be taken up by greater quantities of water. The condensed vapors, however, mixed with the water of condensation, are carried off to the sewer.

Gases passing over with the vapors would presumably be washed in this process; they would not of necessity be made harmless, and the water might be very disagreeable.

Where the gases are burned they are passed directly through the furnace fires and thence up the stack to the open air. They, together with the vapors, are heated to a high degree of temperature, or burned, and float away over the heads of the people, instead of running under their feet, as in the condensation process. If the stacks are high enough and the temperature sufficiently great, these heated vapors will float to a long distance before cooling and descending to an objectionable level. They are probably by that time so mixed with air as to be scarcely appreciable. On damp or rainy days, however, they would undoubtedly be brought to the ground more rapidly than during dry weather.

Sentiment controls largely the complaints which arise on account of garbage.

The householder who properly separates the garbage will not find it more offensive than the soiled plates removed day by day from his table, and if the receptacle was as religiously cleansed as the soiled plates there would be no offensive odors therefrom. Fresh garbage is inoffensive.

Where garbage is collected and permitted to stand in quantities, it is not generally dangerous to life until it becomes putrid. This condition arises, of course, more rapidly during the heat of the summer than at other seasons of the year. Where this garbage is collected in mass and allowed to stand, disinfectants are undoubtedly necessary. This would also be the case where the collections are made, as they are in some cities, at intervals of three days or, when Sunday intervenes, four days apart.

Garbage collected every day can be hauled through the streets without being specially disagreeable to the passer-by. It is not prejudicial to the public health when fresh, and cannot be generally considered so until it makes itself offensive.

Disinfectants in general use are well known—chloride of lime, permanganate of potash, and the dead oils of tar. A very advantageous method of disinfecting both carts and garbage is in use in Buffalo. Creolin, mixed with water, is loaded in a tank charged with compressed air. This tank is fitted with a short hose and spray-nozzle and is attached to the cart. When the cartman finds a receptacle that, in his judgment, needs disinfecting, it is first emptied and then sprayed. The garbage on the cart is then sprayed with the disinfectant. This gives, apparently, very good results.

Dead oils of tar and permanganate of potash are generally used in and about the works and on the floors thereof. The dead oils of tar, on account of their cheapness and because they have no appreciable odor of their own, are in common use.

In the hydrocarbon processes the hydrocarbons used while extracting grease are also well known as disinfectants, naphtha being generally used in the preparation of edible greases. In the mechanical processes, or steam processes, steam itself is a disinfectant. Where rubbish such as tin cans, rags, etc., is disinfected, it is generally done with steam.

Steam at a temperature of 220° F. will destroy all disease germs in four hours' time. Steam under pressure is more valuable, for the reason that it is more penetrating. Steam in motion is also more efficacious than steam at rest.

Heat is the oldest disinfectant known. It is also probably the best, as it is destructive of all organic life.

The driers in general use are cylindrical driers, steam-jacketed, with revolving reels. The shell of the drier is of cast-iron or steel plate. The cast-iron shell is preferable, as it does not erode as rapidly under the action of the gases or the grinding of the material. The shell, also, of cast-iron driers is not subject to leakage, as is frequently the case in steel-plate shells.

The garbage is dried either while fresh or after treatment. Where fresh garbage is shot into the driers, the swill water is advantageous, because it assists in disintegration. Tin cans and other hard refuse, such as crockery, etc., are also advantageous to a certain degree, as they help the revolving paddles to grind the material. It will thus be seen that a cylindrical drier fills three positions when used on fresh garbage: it dries, it grinds, and it cooks. The dried garbage, therefore, is pretty thoroughly cooked and pulverized when it leaves the drier. In general, in this part of the process about sixty per cent. of moisture is driven off.

The operations of driers are continuous. They are loaded from the top and discharged from the bottom. There is no necessity of shutting them down, except for repairs.

When the material is dried after treatment the drier also acts partially as a mill, but in this case no cooking goes on. A certain proportion of foreign substance is also useful in this partial milling process. The work of the drier in this latter case is not so great as where the green garbage is first dried, nor is the wear and tear on the machinery so great, nor is so much heat necessary, as there is a less quantity of moisture to evaporate. As will be readily seen, therefore, the number of driers per ton of garbage would be less than in the former case.

The gases and vapors driven off by the driers go to the condensers or through the furnaces. In cases where cooking is first done, the gases and vapors go from the digesters to the condensers or through the furnaces. The lead pipes to the condensers or furnaces should be of cast-iron, as wrought-iron has not been found satisfactory in actual practice. This is due to the erosive effect of the vapors driven off. It is conclusive, then, that it would be advantageous to have the driers or digesters as close to the furnaces as is practicable.

The extractors and digesters as a rule are of about five tons, capacity, although they are generally considered to hold much more. Whether the overestimate is the fault of the constructors or of the operators, it is difficult to ascertain, as the garbage treated therein varies in proportion of bulk to weight through the different seasons of the year. Constructors are liable to make the extractors as small as possible, on account of the room which they occupy in a building. For this reason their cubic contents may have been, in some instances, decreased.

The operators are desirous of showing as large a capacity in their plant as possible, and therefore may overestimate the weight of green or dried garbage that the extractors hold.

This portion of the machinery is built of varying weights of metal, as different operations and operators use different pressures of steam or naphtha, as the case may be.

In cases where the grease is extracted by pressure the presses inspected have been of the same general character. The results shown are sufficient to indicate that the pressing process, although more rapid than the naphtha process, does not extract so large a percentage of grease. Constant advances are being made in this direction, however, and the presumption is that within a short time much better results will be obtained than at present from the press.

The tankage from the press is generally more noticeable, as far as odor is concerned, than that from the extractor in hydrocarbon or acid processes, the hydrocarbons and acids acting as deodorizers. As this tankage has been thoroughly disinfected by steam boiling, etc., and has been maintained at a temperature above 212° F. for several hours, it is presumably as thoroughly disinfected as in any other case; but there is a stronger odor, which has been so frequently described as that of sweetened coffee, plum-pudding, gingerbread, caramel, etc. The choice of a name depends largely upon the last dinner eaten.

The milling and screening are generally done in separate rooms. The finished product is screened in rotary screens, and the foreign substances and coarse material separated from the fine material. The foreign substances and coarse matter from the screen, generally termed tailings, are separated on the tailing-board. The coarse fertilizer stuff is carried to a mill and ground. The tailings, composed of combustible and non-combustible refuse (but very little of the latter), are burned or thrown away. The product of the mill is mixed with the screened material.

In some cases everything which comes from the drier or extractor goes through the mill, only the coarser and more apparent waste being separated before milling. This gives a more even run of finished tankage, but presumably one that would not show so high an analysis, tankage being sold by analysis—that is, in accordance with the phosphoric acid, potash, and ammonia contained therein.

During the process of milling, care must be taken that the finished product does not ignite. There is so much iron and metal of other kinds in the finished tankage that care has to be observed to prevent firing in the mill. While milling or screening, also, quantities of fine dust are liable to be freed and mixed with the atmosphere. It is this fine dust which carries the odor from the factory, especially if the rooms be not closed and a breeze has an opportunity to get at this dust. It is a question, also, if the insurance companies do not consider that this floating material adds to the risk of insurance. That, together with the naphtha used in some processes and acids in others, would, and probably does, affect the rate of insurance.

The dust from the mill is taken care of in various ways, usually by means of a suction-fan, the mill itself being tightly inclosed. This dust, on analysis, shows a higher per cent. of merchantable products than the milled stuff itself; but it is so small in proportion to the bulk of material handled that it would scarcely pay to collect it.

The screens used are of varying diameters and size of mesh. The rapidity with which they are revolved is also another factor to be considered. They clog chiefly from nails and rags, and it may be found necessary to stop them at intervals in order to free the mesh. These rags, by the by, are a difficult factor in the working of garbage during nearly all stages of the process.

TABLE SHOWING QUANTITY OF GARBAGE PER CAPITA COLLECTED

Buffalo	0.245 lbs. per day	
Boston	0.946 " "	
Wilmington	0.805 " "	
St. Louis	0.277 " "	
New Bedford	0.890 " "	
Cincinnati	0.566 " "	
Philadelphia	0.332 " "	for 3 districts
Lowell	0.408 " "	

TABLE SHOWING AVERAGE COMPOSITION OF GARBAGE AND ITS SELLING VALUE

Three thousand tons of summer garbage, from different cities, treated by different methods, show a general average composition of

Rubbish	7 per cent., or	140 lbs. per ton of garbage
Water	71 " "	1,420 " " "
Grease	2 " "	40 " " "
Tankage	20 " "	400 " " "
	100 " "	2,000 " " "

The selling value of a ton of garbage when thus treated is:

Grease, 40 lbs., at 3 cents		$1.20
Tankage	Ammonia, 13 lbs., at 8 cents	1.04
	Phosphoric acid, 13 lbs., at 1 cent	.13
	Potash, 3 lbs., at 3½ cents	.10
		$2.47

CHAPTER VIII

FINAL DISPOSITION OF STREET-SWEEPINGS AND ASHES

THUS far most of the matters collected by the department carts, with the exception of garbage, have been all dumped together on the scows and taken to sea. The separate treatment of paper and rubbish has been inaugurated, and will before very long become universal, so that it is proposed in this chapter to treat the final disposition of street-sweepings and ashes as it is to be when this shall have been made complete.

At present there are thirteen Barney dumping-boats and a varying number of scows used for this service. The carts collect ashes and street-sweepings at the same time, and dump them together upon the vessels. These are towed to a point beyond the light-ship, some ten miles outside of Sandy Hook, where they are either dumped or unloaded by hand into the sea. When there is a demand for this material for filling (as there happens to be at this writing), so much of it as is called for is loaded on deck-scows and taken by contractors to the lands to be filled, and unloaded by them, the scows being returned to the dumps. The contractor receives for the service a cash sum, which is considerably less than would be the cost to the department of towing to sea.

This whole system is soon to be radically changed. It is proposed to use all of the ashes and sweepings collected

NEAR THE LIGHT-SHIP, SANDY HOOK. UNLOADING DECK-SCOWS WITH FORKS.

About twenty Italians unload the cargo of a deck-scow in about two and one half hours. In 1896 over 760,000 cubic yards of refuse were disposed of in this manner, on 1531 scows, at an average cost of 17.9 cents per cubic yard.

by the department at Riker's Island, in the East River, nearly opposite Morris Point, for filling in a shoal behind a bulkhead constructed for its protection, or for raising the level of the lower part of the land.

Outside of the bulkhead there will be constructed, with suitable piling, a pen or inclosure into which the vessels will be taken, their contents being there dumped. Pumping-machinery will be provided of sufficient capacity to take up the material so dumped and move it in a strong current of water through the pumps and through long pipes or canvas conveyers to the point of deposit. This system for moving earth, etc., has been largely and suc-

A BARNEY DUMPER AT SEA, WITH ITS TUG.

The boat has been opened and is being towed along, the seaway washing out the load. When empty the boat closes by flotation. The department employs a fleet of thirteen Barney dumpers, which in 1896 carried to sea over 1,440,000 cubic yards of refuse, at an average cost of 13.8 cents per cubic yard.

cessfully used on the Potomac Flats at Washington, in government work at League Island, below Philadelphia, and on the Cambridge border of Charles River, near Boston. It was also used in the construction of the North Sea Canal in Holland.

It is proposed to employ for this work a type of vessel

THE DELEHANTY SELF-PROPELLING AUTOMATIC DUMPING-BOAT "CINDERELLA."

of peculiar construction, known as the Delehanty boat. The first of these (the *Cinderella*) is now in successful use for the transportation of sweepings and ashes to sea.

The department is building two other boats of the same character—the *Aschenbroedel* and the *Cendrillon.* Two others, the *Cenerentola* and the *Asschepoester*, are to follow. This fleet of five boats will be adequate for the entire transportation of all of the ashes and sweepings from all parts of the city. It would not be profitable to use them under the present arrangement of direct dumping from carts. Their economical use will require the construction of elevated "pocket-dumps." One such dump is now completed, and is in successful operation at the foot of East Seventeenth Street. When all of the dumping-places are provided with the new structures, the Delehanty boats will be loaded without loss of time, and can make from two to four trips per day to Riker's Island.

The pocket-dump is a steel structure about one hundred feet long and fifty feet high. A continuous link-belt conveyer passes under the pockets, into which the carts are discharged, continues up past one end of the building, returning horizontally under its roof, and down at the other end.

It discharges its material into any one of the ten elevated pockets provided, as may be desired. These pockets have sloping floors and are closed with gates. The gates being opened one after the other, the contents of the pockets fall into the vessel.

The Delehanty boat is a catamaran, or double-hull vessel, with a space twelve feet wide between the two hulls. This space is occupied by pockets rising to a considerable height above the deck. The floors of the pockets are formed of two doors hinged at the sides and opening downward. They are controlled by heavy chains worked by steam-power. When they are released they fall away and the load is delivered, in the case of Riker's

Island inside of the dumping-pit above described. These boats have two propellers with independent engines, are entirely seaworthy, and are easily controlled, so that little time need be lost in placing them under the dumps. The contract price of the Delehanty boat is $40,000. The capacity is about five hundred cubic yards each.

The pocket-dumps cost something less than $20,000 each. There will be at least fifteen such dumps provided for the handling of garbage, sweepings, and ashes only.

The cost of delivering material at Riker's Island and depositing it in place will be about one third of the present cost of sending it to sea. It is estimated that the land thus reclaimed will cost $1400 per acre, and it will be worth at least twice that amount for the city's use.

It is estimated that the fleet of five Delehanty boats (with the shorter trip to Riker's Island) will supplant thirteen Barney dumpers, thirty-five deck-scows, and the equivalent of five tug-boats, in constant use. The cost of these going to the light-ship was, in 1896, $308,600; the cost of transporting the same wastes by the new fleet will be about $96,000; that is, while delivery at Riker's Island will cost only $5\frac{4}{10}$ cents, the cost of delivery at sea is 14 cents, per cubic yard.

CHAPTER IX

FINAL DISPOSITION OF PAPER AND RUBBISH

WE now come to one of the most interesting features of the operations of the department—an outgrowth of the necessity for using hand-labor to "trim the scows." When carts are dumped upon these vessels it is necessary, in order to keep them on an even keel, to employ shovelers to level off the load and distribute it evenly from side to side. This is "scow-trimming."

Some sixteen years ago it cost the city about $11,000 per year for labor. The work was done by Italians, a race with a genius for rag- and bone-picking and for subsisting on rejected trifles of food. These Italians were observed by others to have a job which offered great advantages. Competition arose and continued until, in 1894, when the amount of material delivered at the dumps had greatly increased, the city received for the scow-trimming privilege about $50,000 worth of labor free and more than $90,000 in cash.

The most important item of the scow-trimming recovery then consisted of bones and grease. The paper dumped with the refuse of the streets and ashes became so soiled and wet as to have but little value, and the

LOADING A SCOW WITH REFUSE.

value of even the rags was much reduced by their dirty condition. For nearly a year past we have been collecting paper and rubbish separately, so that rags and paper are much cleaner; and although fully $50,000 worth of bones and fat are now withdrawn in the garbage which is sent to the Utilization Works, the city is still receiving at the rate of about $50,000 for what is left. As paper and rubbish are still dumped upon the ash-scows, much

SORTING THE RAGS AND OTHER ARTICLES OF VALUE UNDER THE OLD-FASHIONED DUMPING-BOARD.

valuable material is lost, and much of what is recovered is more or less soiled.

The system has already been well inaugurated of transporting the paper and rubbish to picking-yards, where it arrives in clean condition, and where all of value that it contains can easily be sorted out, the mere refuse being either burned or, if not combustible, dumped on the scows.

The yard that has been longest in use is that at No. 612 East Eighteenth Street. It contains large sheds for the storing of material, pens for bottles and for tin cans, a "treasury" for the safe-keeping of metals and other trifles of value which would tempt pilferers, and the

TRAVELING BELT AND THE PICKING-GANG.

machinery that is used in connection with the work. This consists mainly of a traveling belt about eighty feet long, which rises out of a shallow pit into which the contents of the carts are thrown, and runs horizontally for fifty feet between two rows of workmen, each engaged in selecting the kind of paper, rag, or other material to which he is assigned. The belt rises on a steep angle to the mouth of the furnace, where straw, excelsior, bits of wood, and worthless paper are burned. In connection with this furnace there is a large steam-boiler, which

THE BELT RISING TO THE FEED-DOOR OF THE FURNACE.

furnishes the power for moving the belt, and from which, thus far, a great amount of steam under high pressure is going to waste. When means are found for utilizing this waste steam still further economy will result. This yard receives daily about fifty large loads of all manner of refuse which householders, storekeepers, manufacturers, and others wish to get rid of. The average sales per week during the months of July and August were as follows:

Paper	$128.40
Rags	89.37
Other materials	43.47
Total	$261.24

This is for the collections of ten carts of the one hundred and fifty in use. It is only a general indication. The outlook is that the returns will increase.

The second yard is being provided with a belt and small engine only, all wastes being sent to the scows, and no account being taken of steam. Still another yard is being arranged, where a vastly greater burning capacity will be furnished, and where it is thought that two hundred loads per day can be handled.

The experiments with these three yards will enable us to determine which is the more advantageous method to be adopted, and especially to decide the very important question as to whether this work shall be done in a large number of yards within the city, or whether all of the paper and rubbish shall be transported to Riker's Island, there to be picked over and sorted in one large establishment, for which ample space can be furnished. The saving in rent would be very great, and the present indications are that this and the simpler and more economical administration will outweigh the cost of transportation.

It is impossible to say what will be the amount to be received by the city as a profit on these operations; but there are already indications that the easy facility afforded to householders to get rid of all manner of wastes is leading them to discard more and more of things that they have hitherto thought worth saving. That the profit will greatly exceed any amount hitherto received for scow-trimming is already demonstrated.

CHAPTER X

STOCK AND PLANT

BY MAJOR H. C. CUSHING, ASSISTANT SUPERINTENDENT

WHEN the Department of Street-Cleaning came under its present administration the plant was inadequate and in bad condition. This was particularly the case in the matter of carts, harness, and horses. Of the first two items many were out of repair and showed a lack of systematic care. A great many of the horses were low in flesh and of a class unfitted for their peculiar work, being large and long-legged. Such animals, when once they get reduced, are very difficult to recuperate. A new standard was determined on, and the horses purchased thereafter were typical cart-horses, and of such uniform excellence that the expert judges who have passed on the merits of the various stables at the annual parades have stated that it would seem hardly possible to assemble together such an even lot.

The stables were deficient in the necessary supplies, and were run in a very loose way as to discipline. They were the resort of the local politicians, and the foremen were at the mercy of these. If an inefficient employee was laid off or discharged, all he had to do was to go to his ward leader to get himself reinstated. This was a serious drawback to discipline, for the stable foremen could not do what was proper without prejudicing their own positions. The very first thing, then, that was done was to change the existing conditions entirely. Every one in the service, from the highest to the lowest, was given to understand that his position implied work according to his responsibility; that so long as he did that work his personal opinions and politics would not be considered; and that the stables must no longer be a lounging-place for outsiders. A system of day-and-night inspection was inaugurated, and at inopportune periods the higher officials would drop down on a stable, often discovering some one absent or neglecting his duty.

After preliminary warning, men who were proved to be persistent offenders were discharged and their places filled by better men. The stable employees soon found that all they had to do was to attend to business. New material was obtained as fast as possible, that on hand was repaired, a sufficient force was placed in each stable to keep it in order, and a spirit of rivalry was encouraged. The result is that to-day, on the testimony of some of the largest and most experienced liverymen, there are no public stables run in a more systematic manner than those of the department, nor kept in as fine condition. One of these gentlemen went so far as to say that he doubted if there were ten private stables in New York which, in all the essentials of stable management, could excel them.

This result has been secured by the rigid application of systematic rules and, furthermore, by the encouragement of special prizes of banners, etc., given to those stables which, both in the care of the equipment and the condition of the animals, exhibited the most merit. After the first annual parade, which demonstrated so markedly the condition of the department, it was resolved to send a cart from each stable for exhibition at the National Horse-show. This innovation at such a fashionable function was a decided success and added much to the increasing popularity of the department, besides greatly raising the *esprit de corps* of the drivers.

This, in general terms, shows how the condition and morale of the stable department have been raised. There are nine stables in all, situated in convenient parts of the city, near the water-front, and from Hamilton Street on the south to One Hundred and Fifty-second Street on the north. One of these, Stable A, in addition to being a stable is the great depot and repair-shop. To it all new stock is brought, horse-dealers bring their horses for examination and purchase, and broken carts, etc., are sent for repair. It is a very busy place. The other eight are purely stables, and only the ordinary harness-repairing and simple work on vehicles are done at them.

All horses are shod by contract, at a fixed price per month. There are three veterinary surgeons on duty daily. The assistant superintendent has general charge of all stables and of the carting force. He is responsible for the condition of the men and of the stock; he is also charged with the carrying out of all disciplinary rules affecting drivers. His immediate assistant is the superintendent of stables, whose duties are such as are implied by his title. A regular system of reports and returns, affecting both the personnel and the material, has been inaugurated, similar in all its essential details to that of the army. Each stable has a foreman, an assistant foreman, clerks, and hostlers. In addition thereto there are various stablemen to cleanse harness and carts and to do the usual work. The number of these depends on the capacity of the stable, i. e., so many horses to the man. This force takes entire care of the horses.

The ash-cart-driver is not required to do anything more than to hitch up his team and unhitch it when he returns. The morning hitching up is very rapidly and systematically done. The carts are grouped in the stable according to the sections they work in. When the bell sounds for roll-call, drivers fall in by sections, immediately proceed to the stall floors, harness and lead their horses to the cart floor, hitch up, and start off for daily work. Frequently the whole force of a large stable has been timed as getting out to work in ten minutes or thereabouts. After the drivers leave the stable, and until they return thereto at night, they are controlled by the district superintendents. Their work is of a variable nature. On the outset they remove a portion of the ashes, for their second load they take away the garbage, and on the last round the street-sweepings. It depends a good deal on circumstances as to how long they are employed during the day, but no driver may return to the stable until he has cleaned up his route. Nor must he mix one of the above classes of material with another. At noon he has a lay-off or swing of from one and a half to two hours. During the day the various officers are moving about the streets, and when a driver is found derelict in his duty he is reported to the main office for proper punishment. A specific code of rules governs him, and he knows exactly what to expect for violation thereof. The lot of a driver is hard as compared with that of a sweeper.

The latter simply sweeps the street, collects the rubbish in bags or piles, and his work is done. The driver has to collect all this refuse; has to have animated conflicts with janitors, servants, saloon-keepers, etc., as to whether their garbage is garbage or their refuse material "proper"; and, finally, has to satisfy exacting foremen by not *loitering*, and critical dump-inspectors as to the character of his loads. Then, he must not enter a saloon, nor trot his horse, nor do many things. For all that, the position of driver is quite popular. It is wider and more varied in its experiences than that of the staid and respectable sweeper, who is confined to one restricted locality. A driver of a convivial or amatory turn has hazardous opportunities to get a surreptitious drink, and can occasionally indulge in a brief flirtation.

There are two classes of drivers—regulars and extras. The latter are eligible for work only when a regular is absent or sick. There are generally about twenty or thirty extra drivers on the list at each stable available to be called on. Drivers are uniformed in brown canvas suits, with brown helmets. It would be impossible for them to use the white uniform of the sweeper. The same general system as regards the organization and discipline above noted of the stable force obtains with the sweeper force and the mechanic force.

To carry on the operations of a department which has arisen to such importance and which deals with so many problems requires a variety of employees, each of special aptitude, from the sweeper who manipulates his broom and the driver who handles his ash-can in a workmanlike manner, up to the scientific expert who deals with abstruse sanitary problems. All have their specified work, and all are held to a rigid accountability in the performance of it; and the commissioner holds himself to as rigid an accountability as any.

Furthermore, the carrying on of this business necessitates a large plant—stables, repair-shops, section stations, as well as incumbrance-yards where derelict trucks are impounded, yards where the refuse is sorted for sale, dumps, scows, etc. Incidental to all this there must be special men employed as inspectors to keep a watchful eye on everything, and whose timely reports may be considered as the lubricant which makes all the various wheels turn around in unison.

The department is divided into five great divisions: (1) the sweepers, under the control of the general superintendent; (2) the stables and drivers, under the assistant superintendent; (3) final disposition, under the superintendent of final disposition; (4) the mechanics, under the master mechanic; and (5) the clerical force, under the chief clerk. The sweepers are directly under the control of district superintendents and section foremen. The drivers are under the same control while out on their work. The city is divided into eleven districts and sixty-five sections. Each two sections have their section station, where the sweepers assemble in the morning to be sent to work, and where the brooms, watering-cans, etc., are kept. There the men leave their ordinary clothes and assume their white uniforms. These section stations are kept in fine order, and are a vast improvement over the old assembling-places at the street-corner.

The superintendent of final disposition controls the movements of the various dump-boats and the final disposition of all the refuse. This in winter is sometimes a very serious problem.

Lastly, there is the snow-inspector, a district superintendent detailed for the winter who directs the removal of snow and ice and supervises the contractors who attend to it.

The clerical force at the main office is under the direction of the chief clerk. Its employees come from the civil service, and are engaged in various classes of clerical work and the preparation of statistics. This bureau, while not impressing itself so markedly on the general public as those above cited, is a very important one, as may well be imagined.

Having thus given a general idea of the various departments and duties, it is only necessary to recapitulate in the tabular form all the information as to personnel and material in the main items to enable the reader to understand what an important department this is; and it here follows:

TABULATED STATEMENT OF THE CONDITION OF THE DEPARTMENT OF STREET-CLEANING, CITY OF NEW YORK, JUNE 13, 1897

MISCELLANEOUS

Grade	Pay Day Month Year	Force Officers	Force Men	Specific Duties
Commissioner	$6000 Y.	1		Controls everything.
Deputy commissioner	4000 Y.	1		Assists commissioner; makes purchases.
Chief clerk	3600 Y.	1		Charge of clerical force.
Gen. superintendent	3000 Y.	1		General executive; charge particularly of sweepers.
Asst. superintendent	2500 Y.	1		General executive; charge of stables and drivers.
Supt. of stables	2000 Y.	1		Special supervision of stables.
Supt. of final disposition	2000 Y.	1		Charge of dumps, scows, and refuse.
Assistant supt. of final disposition	1500 Y.	1		Assistant to above.
Master mechanic	1800 Y.	1		Charge of mechanics, construction, repairs.
Private secretary	1500 Y.	1		Charge of commissioner's correspondence, etc.
Time-collectors	1200 Y.	3		Collect time-books; also special inspectors.
Total miscellaneous		13		

CLERICAL FORCE

Grade	Pay Day Month Year	Force Officers	Force Men	Specific Duties
General bookkeeper	$1750 Y.	1		Bookkeeping.
Assistant	900 Y.		1	
Supt. pay-rolls	1750 Y.	1		Pay-rolls.
Assistants	900 Y.		5	
Application and registration clerk	1800 Y.	1		Registration of applications for position.
Incumbrance and contract clerk	2000 Y.	1		Charge of seizures made for incumbrance, and of contracts and legal business.
Stenographers and type-writers	360 to 1500 Y.		4	Duties indicated.
Complaint clerk	1000 Y.	1		Attends to complaints.
Property clerk	1800 Y.	1		Charge of property stored at main depot.
General clerks	1500 to 900 Y.		6	Clerical work.
Total clerical force		6	16	

SWEEPER FORCE

Grade	Pay	Officers	Men	Specific Duties
District superintendents	1800 Y.	11		Charge of districts.
Section foremen	1260 Y.	58		Charge of sections.
Assistant section foremen	900 Y.		167	Assist in charge of sections, detailed men, and various duties.
Regular sweepers	600 Y. 660 Y. 720 Y.		1614	Sweeping streets.
Total sweeper force		69	1781	
Extra sweepers	2.00 D.		219	Employed temporarily to replace absent sweepers.

DRIVER FORCE

Grade	Pay	Officers	Men	Specific Duties
Stable foremen	1300 Y.	9		Charge of stables.
Assistant stable foremen	1000 Y.	11		Assist in charge of stables.
Hostlers	720 Y.		92	Grooming horses, etc.
Regular drivers	600 Y. 660 Y. 720 Y.		893	Driving carts, collecting refuse, and detailed work in stables and elsewhere.
Total driver force		20	985	
Extra drivers	2.00 D.		249	Employed temporarily to replace absent drivers.

FINAL DISPOSITION

Grade	Pay Day Month Year	Force Officers	Force Men	Specific Duties
Dump-inspectors	$1200 Y.	17		Charge of dumps.
Assistant dump-inspectors	900 Y.	16		Assist in charge of dumps.
Tug- and scow-inspectors	1200 Y.	19		Charge of tugs and scows.
Masters	110 M.	1		On board of *Cinderella*.
Mates	60 M.	1		" " "
Engineers	100 M.	1		" " "
Assistant	60 M.		1	" " "
Firemen	40 M.		2	" " "
Deck-hands	40 M.		1	" " "
Cooks	30 M.		1	" " "
Total final disposition		55	5	

MECHANIC FORCE

Mechanics	2.50 D. 3.25 D.	76	General mechanical work.
Mechanics' helpers	2.00 D. 2.50 D.	6	General mechanical work.
Total mechanic force		82	

RECAPITULATION

	Officers	Men
Miscellaneous	13	
Clerical force	6	16
Sweeper force	69	1781
Driver force	20	985
Final disposition	55	5
Mechanic force		82
Grand total	163	2869

Officers and men	3032
Extra sweepers and drivers	468
All told, regulars and extras	3500

MATERIAL AND PLANT

SWEEPERS' DEPARTMENT, AUGUST 31

Article, Animal, Property, etc.	Number
Bicycles	75
Brooms	5,141
Bags	30,769

SWEEPERS' DEPARTMENT, AUGUST 31—CONTINUED

ARTICLE, ANIMAL, PROPERTY, ETC.	NUMBER
Bag-carriers	1,355
Cans, ash-	681
Cans, sprinkling-	2,007
Cans, paper-, fruit-	83
Carts, hoky-poky	20
Hose	3,138
Receptacles	207
Incumbrance-yards	2
Section stations	41

DRIVERS' DEPARTMENT, AUGUST 31

Ash-carts	875
Ash-trucks	6
Wagons	13
Light wagons	31
Sweeping-machines	18
Water-carts	33
Paper-carts	150
Trucks	10
Snow-plows, etc.	20
Hose-carts	10
Harness sets	1,316
Horses	945
Stables	9

FINAL DISPOSITION, AUGUST 31

Dumps	14
Barney dump-boats, hired	13
Delehanty dump-boat	1
Scows	22
Crematory	1
Stake-boat	1
Tug-boats, hired	4

H. C. C.

CHAPTER XI

THE REMOVAL OF SNOW

BY H. L. STIDHAM, SNOW-INSPECTOR

THE removal of snow has always presented one of the most vexatious problems confronting the various administrations. The removal of "new-fallen snow from leading thoroughfares and such other streets and avenues as may be found practicable" is a duty made obligatory upon the commissioner by law, and with each year the moral obligation to the vast traffic interests of congested Manhattan Island becomes more insistent. Of late, also, the question of the health of the community has entered with great force into any consideration of the subject. With the crowding of the immense tenement population into that human beehive, the East Side, there has been an actual bulging out from the houses to the now clean asphalt streets. Whether it be winter or summer, the people must have this additional room opened up for them, and a delay in the removal of the almost knee-deep snow and befouled slush is at the cost of much sickness, and probably many lives, each winter.

With such an uncertain quantity to estimate upon as the yearly snowfall, the annual appropriations for this important part of the department's work have been nominal sums of $25,000 or $40,000. Between the years 1882 and 1892 the annual expenditure was never more than $45,000, and averaged nearly within the $25,000 allowed. In the past three years, with the enormous increase in the amounts of snow removed, there has necessarily been a much larger annual expenditure. Any sums needed beyond the yearly appropriation are transferred from other department accounts by the Board of Estimate and Apportionment, and are afterward replaced by the sale of revenue bonds.

In the small amounts of snow removed each winter up to January, 1895, the work was performed mainly with the regular department force, hiring additional laborers and carts when the fall was a heavy one.

The quantity of street area opened to traffic by this method was necessarily insignificant, and was centered in a small portion of the down-town districts. Here nearly all the sweepers from the various sections throughout the entire city were concentrated into piling and loading gangs, and the department carts in use in the hauling of ashes and garbage during the day were sent, with fresh horses and drivers, to the snow district for the night duty, which constituted nearly all the work.

In the early months of 1895 the removal by day's work was continued, but, for the first time, each of the eleven districts did its own work, and its head was made responsible for the hiring of most of the additional carts and laborers required. In this the first year of the present administration the work was extended materially, and the mileage of streets cleared increased in all parts of the city, with the securing of many more hired carts than were ever used before.

In the autumn of 1895–96 the first proposal for the removal of snow and ice by contract was advertised for, and the contract was let to the only bidder, Herbert Tate, at 56 cents per cubic yard. No snow was removed under this agreement until after the first of the year 1896.

With the beginning of 1896 a new era began. Quantities hitherto undreamed of were removed in every storm, and the mileage of cleared streets increased enormously. The work was done by the contractor in the manner and at the places ordered, and a temporary bureau was organized and placed in entire charge of the burdensome details that had so long hampered the regular department work. Because of the letting of the contract in cubic yards, it was necessary to arrange for inspectors at the loading- and dumping-places, to tally the loads and to protect the city's interests. All cartmen had to get their loads from the regular loading-places and dump them into the river before receiving the token of the city's indebtedness. Under the contract system, the department was relieved entirely of the care and labor incident to the hiring of carts and men, keeping their time and making up pay-rolls; and the vexatious delays in payment of the emergency forces formerly attending the removal of snow were obviated altogether. The contractor, by paying both cartmen and shovelers promptly after each storm, made possible the removal of the present extraordinary and constantly increasing daily totals. The department laborers were retained in their own sections upon the necessary cross-walk and gutter work, and the interruptions to the regular department routine were reduced to a minimum. Snow removal became a mere matter of dollars and cents. Much better results were secured (by the contractor paying by the load) from the limited supply of vehicles at the disposal of the city. The drivers, instead of hauling eight or ten loads for a day's work and then leaving, as formerly, worked continuously and as rapidly as their horses could be made to move, in the endeavor to get in as many loads, and therefore secure as much money, as possible.

In the autumn of 1896 there were three bidders for the contract for the season of 1896–97, and it was let to G. M. Furman for 42 cents per cubic yard. It will be seen from the table below that the amount of snow removed under this contract is considerably more than the totals for both of the two previous winters.

The table shows for every winter the official snowfall in inches, the number of loads removed by the department forces and by the respective contractors, the totals for each winter, with the total cost and the cost per load. (A load of snow is taken as one and one half cubic yards.) The second column comprises the day's work of the department in every winter, and in addition the removal by Contractor Tate for 1895–96 and by Contractor Furman for 1896–97. The third column shows the amounts removed by the contractors who, from 1882 to 1888 inclusive, had entire charge of the street-cleaning work below Fourteenth Street, and were compelled by their contract to cart away snow without extra cost to the city. In the fourth column likewise is given, wherever the separation could be made, the number of loads removed each winter after that of 1885–86 by Holland & Co., who cart away all the snow on Broadway from Bowling Green to Park Place for the Metropolitan Street-Railway Company, without expense to the city.

Neither of these columns, then, the third and fourth, although included in the totals by winters, enters into the costs of removal, which are made up solely from the bills presented for the work done by department forces and Contractors Tate and Furman, as shown in the second column. These costs, also, are all exclusive of supervision by the department inspectors, foremen, and superintendents.

Winters.	Snowfall in inches.	Loads by day's work, department forces, and Contractors Tate and Furman.	Loads by the contractors below Fourteenth Street.	Loads by Holland & Co., lower Broadway.	Totals.	Total cost per winter.	Cost per load.
1881–82	. .	*23,174	. .	. .	*23,174	*$22,551.24	*$.973
1882–83	. .	18,475	17,927	. .	36,402	15,360.04	.831
1883–84	. .	40,709	30,124	. .	70,833	27,352.05	.672
1884–85	36.6	22,313	18,195	. .	40,508	20,213.22	.906
1885–86	23.9	21,578	26,807	. .	48,385	15,035.24	.697
1886–87	49.5	30,973	32,203	1,332	64,508	24,429.53	.789
1887–88	47.4	51,894	18,320	5,886	76,100	47,474.40	.915
1888–89	21.9	4,010	No snow was hauled by these contractors after 1887–88.	1,086	5,096	5,985.22	1.493
1889–90	34.1	36,359		402	36.761	29,555.82	.813
1890–91	39.5	64,132		. .	64,132	56,405.53	.880
1891–92	36.5	27,052		. .	27,052	23,094.28	.854
1892–93	77.6	86,213		. .	86,213	62,458.78	.724
1893–94	56.1	105,669		. .	105,669	60,691.51	.574
1894–95, up to January 15	11.4	64,074		1,260	65,334	42,498.93	.663
1894–95, after January 15	24.8	261,884		1,825	263,709	183,225.64	.700
1895–96	42.0	271,265		1,980	273,245	254,716.65	.939
1896–97	39.1	700,263		2,726	702,989	445,038.59	.636

It will be noted that in the above table the winter of 1894–95 is divided into two portions—the one before January 15, 1895, and the other after that date. In the summary of the table these portions, for the sake of

* These figures are the only ones found in the "City Record," but the total in loads is 5137 less than the number given in Commissioner Coleman's "Review of the Operations of the Department," published in 1889.

convenience, are each called a half of a winter. The summary is shown below, and is a comparison of the period from 1881 to 1895, under previous commissioners, with that of the present administration since its inauguration on January 15, 1895. It gives the totals by day's work and by contract, and the entire amounts of snow removed for the periods mentioned. The average number of loads for a winter in each period, with their comparative percentages, the total cost of removal, and the average cost per cart-load, are also shown.

SUMMARY

Periods.	Loads by day's work, department forces, and Contractors Tate and Furman.	Loads by contractors below Fourteenth Street, and on lower Broadway.	Total number of loads for entire period.	Average per winter in loads.	Relative percentage of averages by winters.	Total cost of removal.	Average cost per load.
From winter 1881–82 to January 15, 1895, equals 13½ winters	596,625	153,542	750,167	55,568	11.2	$453,105.79	$.759
January 15, 1895, to spring, 1897, equals 2½ winters	1,233,412	6,531	1,239,943	495,977	100	882,980.88	.716

It will be seen from this summary that the amount of snow removed in the two complete winters, 1895–96 and 1896–97, and in the portion of 1894–95, is 1,239,943 loads (one and one half cubic yards each), almost twice the entire amount removed in the thirteen full winters and the portion of another before January 15, 1895. The average per winter for the present administration is 495,977 loads, against 55,568 loads for the winters preceding. The total cost of removal under all the former commissioners is $453,105.79, or an average cost per load removed of $.759; under the present administration it has been $882,980.88, or an average cost per load of $.716. This is over four cents lower than the average for all the previous administrations, and would be much smaller were it not for the fact that the first contract price, 56 cents per cubic yard, or 84 cents per load, was high—only one contractor risking an entirely untried and venturesome experiment even at that figure. Another reason for the increased cost in 1895–96 is that in that winter the wages of the large sweeping force engaged in the cleaning of cross-walks, opening of gutters, etc., were charged to the snow and ice account. This has not been done in 1896–97.

Another and most important point that should be borne in mind in the consideration of any question of cost is the well-known fact that the standard of the size of loads set in the years 1895, 1896, and 1897 is far more exacting than was ever attempted before.

As showing most markedly the great increase in the amount of snow removed, the following paragraph from the report of Commissioner Coleman for 1888 is subjoined:

"A snow-storm of unequaled severity broke over this city on March 12, 1888. By reason of its intensity and violence it is popularly known and referred to as the 'blizzard.' The amount of the snowfall was unprecedented, being, according to official figures, twenty-two inches, and threatened to affect the business of the city to an alarming extent. To meet this emergency the physical and financial resources of this department were fully tested. The appropriation for the removal of snow and ice for the whole year was only $25,000, and the greater part of that sum had already been expended for work done in January and February. But this department made no delay in addressing itself to the great task which so unexpectedly confronted it, and worked so rapidly that the threatened blockade of the streets and stoppage of business were soon averted. Traffic in the commercial districts, which had been temporarily suspended, was speedily resumed, and before the expiration of one week almost all traces of the memorable snow-storm had been practically effaced from the streets."

The total amount of snow actually removed during the work on this huge storm, as given by the same report, is 40,542 loads. This includes the amount removed with the department forces by day's work, the amount removed by the contractors below Fourteenth Street, and the amount carted away by the contractor hauling for the Metropolitan Street-Railway Company on lower Broadway.

In *every* storm of the past winter there were well over 200,000 loads, and on one day alone 55,773 loads were hauled, exclusive of railroad work and the lower Broadway contract. This is 15,000 more than the total for the entire week's work on the "blizzard." An average of the ten largest days' work for the winter of 1896–97 gives 40,534 loads.

A comparison of the mileage of streets cleared per

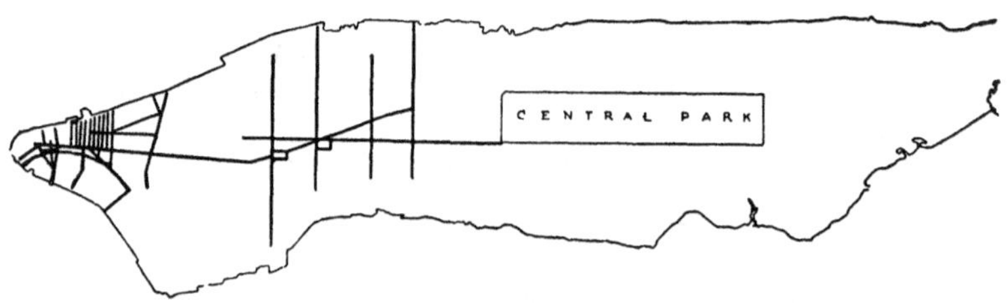

STREETS CLEANED OF SNOW IN AVERAGE STORM, PRIOR TO 1895. MILEAGE, 22.80.

storm is also of interest. The accompanying map of the city shows the streets, in full black, cleared during the work upon an average storm in the period preceding this administration. The mileage is 22.80—a fair, if not too large, average for the storms of varying depth and under different commissioners.

The second map here given shows the streets (marked in full black, as before) cleared in the storm from February 12 to February 16, inclusive, 1897. Virtually all the street area below Houston Street received attention. About one half of the streets between Houston and Fifty-ninth streets were cleared of snow, and above Fifty-ninth Street the main traffic thoroughfares and some of the crowded tenement streets. The mileage of this storm is 144.416, one and one half miles less than the average for the winter, the snowfalls in which were all unusually heavy.

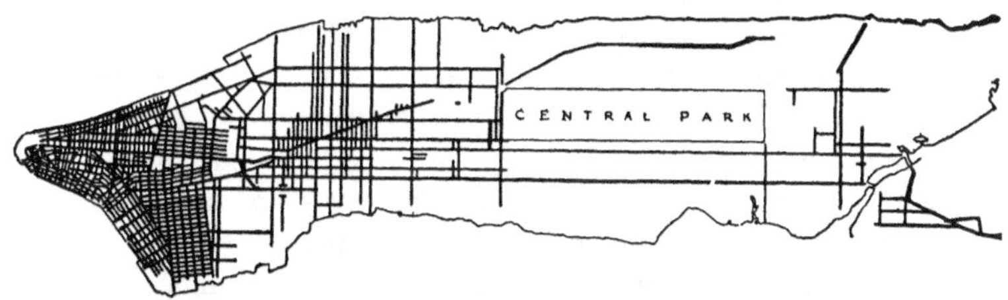

STREETS CLEANED OF SNOW, FEBRUARY 12 TO FEBRUARY 16, 1897.
MILEAGE, 144.42.

A very marked difference between the two maps will be noticed in looking at the congested tenement district east of the Bowery and south of Houston Street. This was never touched formerly, while now it is virtually entirely cleared in every storm.

A most important feature of the snow work has been

the agreements made with the street-railways. Under an opinion from the counsel to the corporation, the commissioner of street-cleaning has been authorized to enter into agreements with the various street-railways in the city for the amount of snow removal to be performed by them in lieu of that required under the provisions of Section 271, Chapter VIII., Revised Ordinances. This ordinance demands, upon the part of the companies, that they cart away all snow thrown off their tracks by their plows or sweeping-machines. A definite arrangement has been made with all the companies, each assuming the entire responsibility for a certain fixed street area, from curb to curb, instead of only on its tracks, while the city clears the snow from as much of the remainder of the streets through which the company's tracks pass as is deemed practicable and necessary.

Before the inauguration of the present system of removal by contract the procedure was, as already explained, to hire extra carts and laborers by the day to assist the regular department force. Permission had first to be obtained from the mayor to hire such additional help, and it had to be renewed at the expiration of every three days. Before the winter of 1894–95 the hiring of these emergency laborers was done indirectly through certain bosses or "padrones," controlling a large number of men each. The padrone received from the city $1.50 per day for each laborer furnished, and retained from this sum a small percentage as compensation for his own services. He paid his men daily upon the completion of their work, although the city's payment in wages was never received by him until some time after each storm. No matter how sudden the call for laborers, they were furnished at once and in any number desired. Moreover, they were all picked men, young and robust, and accustomed to the heaviest manual labor. They were chosen without reference to their citizenship.

Strong pressure was brought to bear upon the State legislature of 1894 by the labor-unions of this city, and a law was passed amending the Consolidation Act so that any extra laborers thereafter to be employed by the Department of Street-Cleaning in the removal of snow, as well as in the regular department work, were to be American citizens and residents of the city. They were to be paid not less than $2 for eight hours' work, and were to be chosen only from an eligible list of men passing a certain physical examination.

Thus the opening of the winter of 1894–95 saw the padrone system done away with, an increase of one third in the wages to be paid for labor, and the initiation of complicated and burdensome machinery for the hiring and paying of the emergency forces.

The first two storms after the present commissioner took office were less than two inches in depth and were followed by warm weather. The department forces and their hired helpers worked rapidly, but very much more snow melted off than was removed. Despite this patent fact, a vast amount of unintelligent praise and undeserved encomium hailed these first efforts at snow removal. These thoughtless pæans of the press were changed into equally hasty and unfounded criticisms after the storm of February 7 and 8—a fall of five and a half inches, which was followed almost immediately by unusually severe and prolonged cold weather. The snow obstinately remained on the streets, and the department worked continuously for fourteen days in its removal.

During that time 128.59 miles of streets in different sections of the city were cleared.

The department was deluged with suggestions, ranging from the flushing of the streets (with the thermometer hovering about zero!) to the use of melting-machines. A number of experiments were conducted with different appliances, but only two—the one with a naphtha melting-machine and the other with a steam-pit—held out any hopes of even moderate value. In the latter, a trial concrete vault, eight by two by five feet, with a steam-pipe at the bottom, kept covered always with a foot of water, and with an outlet connection to the nearest sewer, was constructed on Franklin Street. Steam was supplied by means of an ordinary boiler mounted on a four-wheel truck alongside the pit. The experiments were a practical failure—the snow shoveled into the pit melting very slowly, and the pit soon becoming choked with dirt.

As regards the record of the department under the new administration, it more than held its own in the eyes of every fair-minded citizen when figures were adduced showing that the various commissioners during the five *years* beginning with 1889 had removed 221,569 loads of snow, at a total cost of $178,737.34, while there were removed, in the five *weeks* under the new direction, 253,481 loads, at a cost of $173,839.20. In this short time, then, more snow was removed, at less expense, than in the entire five years prior to the present administration, notwithstanding the fact that the department had to pay $2 per day for labor, where former commissioners secured theirs for $1.50.

In a communication at the time the commissioner summarized the whole deplorable situation in the statement that the delay in paying "lay entirely at the door of organized labor," and showed how much better off the men would be under the contract system, with their somewhat smaller daily wage paid immediately. Many of the shovelers worked only one day, earning $2, and the average for all men working on the last four days of the January storm was only $3.26. For this pittance the 5028 men who had earned it had to stand around in the cold or wet, day after day, to get their money. Counting the time spent in coming for their pay, these innocent victims of an iniquitous law earned not more than 50 cents per day. Instead of receiving 50 cents per day *more* than their services were worth in the open market, they actually earned only one third of their old wages. In other words, the department appeared, as compared with the former padrone, in the light of an unwieldy concern, whose cumbersome machinery and necessary red tape caused its temporary employees to work fewer hours than either they or the city desired, and not only to receive far less money, but to be compelled to wait for it.

To one who remarks the ease with which over 50,000 loads of snow are now removed daily under the contract system, it is remarkable to look back upon the strain under which all officials, from the highest to the lowest, passed the entire winter only two years ago. From the 18th of January to and including the 21st of February, the work of snow removal was prosecuted with but the intermission of seven days when no outside work was done. The district superintendents and section foremen worked on snow removal during the night and until three or four o'clock in the morning, and then reported bright and early the next day for the regular work of removing ashes and garbage, the supervision of sweepers, etc. This unceasing toil was kept up day after day, and even the clerical force worked twice its usual hours. Certain it is that, since the relief afforded by the contract system, the department will never again see such a severe and long-continued strain, and in the future most of its officials, as was the case during the winter just past, will be left free to attend to the routine work normally heavy in every winter.

In the event of a snowfall the contractor has ample time to get his immense organization in readiness for the commissioner's order to begin removal. Usually this is not given until the snow ceases, unless the storm is seen to be a heavy one.

When the order is received, operations are begun within a few hours in every district from the Battery to north of the Harlem River, and almost simultaneously in each. The contractor's trusted subordinates collect large numbers of the unemployed at certain fixed meeting-places, and gangs are formed of pilers and shovelers. Owners of carts and wagons in any number have already been told at the beginning of the season where to report in the event of a snow-storm, and at any time during the removal a man with a vehicle of the required capacity is put to work immediately upon application. There are always more shovelers applying than can be given employment, but never enough carts.

The points at which the work is begun are fixed, and the schedules remain the same for each storm. These points are chosen as far as possible with regard to their relative importance, but with due consideration to the practical problem of keeping the gangs well separated, at equal distances from the river-front, and in such positions that the hauling to the dumps may be fairly equalized according to the capacity of each.

At each loading-place is a department foreman, who, after a cart has been loaded from the street in which the work is being conducted, and if the load is satisfactory in size, gives to the driver a coupon signifying that the snow has been taken under department supervision. At the piers used as dumping-points the loaded carts move out to the extreme end along one side; the drivers dump their snow over the string-pieces into the river, and submit to the inspection of department subordinates, who see that the carts are entirely emptied, that no snow is dumped on the pier, and that no false loads are allowed for. The empty carts return down the pier in single file on the opposite side, passing a department foreman at the street end, who receives from the driver his loading coupon, and hands to a representative of the contractor, standing by his side, an equivalent brass check, properly stamped and numbered, as a tally of the city's indebtedness. The driver then receives a voucher from the contractor's representative, showing that a load of snow has been regularly hauled and dumped, and that pay for the same will be given upon presentation of the voucher at the contractor's main offices. This is negotiable, as is also the similar voucher for hours of labor performed which is handed to each shoveler at the close of his day's work; and both are honored, to the bearer upon demand, at any time afterward.

The number of brass checks turned in each day by the various representatives of the contractor is credited to his account by the snow-inspector, and constitutes the basis of the bills presented by him for cubic yards removed.

The above outline will serve to indicate general methods, and it is not necessary to describe the numberless details connected with the administration of the work, all of which, however, are felt very forcibly in the labor incident to the removal of over 75,000 cubic yards and the clearing of 30 miles of streets daily.

After the first storm of the winter, for which the department and the contractor were both unprepared, the system of inspection was practically perfect. The loading and dump foremen were exceedingly strict, and the loads hauled were much larger than ever before. The reports of the various inspectors and detectives were most encouraging, and not a suspicion of dishonesty attached itself to any of the transactions incident to the loading and dumping. The controller's representative was given every facility in his inspections in all the districts, and expressed the highest appreciation of the manner in which the city's interests were being guarded.

A number of experiments for the purpose of devising new methods, reducing costs, etc., were conducted during the winter. Plows and the Hudson River ice-scrapers (for asphalt streets) were used freely wherever the results warranted. In heavy storms the plows serve to clear a passageway in the street until removal can be secured. The scrapers are of most service in piling ahead of the loading gangs in light falls.

The attempts to use sweeping-machines, with specially prepared brooms, proved unqualified failures, even when begun as soon as the snow commenced falling.

On Madison Avenue, from Twenty-third to Forty-second streets, the snow was scraped to the middle of the street and piled in long ridges, with an opening in the center of each block for vehicles. It was then allowed to remain, with the hope that it would disappear through natural causes. It was found, however, that the alternate melting and freezing caused thin runnels of ice from the ridge to the curb on each side, which made the street almost impassable late in the afternoon and at night, and the department was forced to cart away the snow.

On the Boulevard from Fifty-ninth to One Hundred and Twelfth streets, in the last two storms, the snow was not removed, but was pushed from the parkway in the center toward the curb on each side and there piled into ridges. The street was thus opened to traffic promptly and with very little expense. No ice formed, as in the Madison Avenue experiment, because the drainage was not across the cleared pavement. The only disadvantage of the method was perceived some time after each storm, when the snow had melted from all the neighboring streets and the Boulevard was left with a black, dirty ridge on either side for its entire length. This was remedied by scattering out.

In the last storm of the season the rapidity with which the Boulevard was opened up to bicycling and traffic by this method is deserving of mention. Although the snow did not cease falling until Friday night, and the storm was a heavy one, by Sunday morning the entire length of this popular thoroughfare from Fifty-ninth Street to One Hundred and Twelfth Street was perfectly clean and dry, and was traversed by hundreds of bicycles and carriages.

On all the asphalt and some of the stone streets cleared the contractor used the steel-pan scrapers (for asphalt sweeping) behind his carts, scraping the thin, dirty residue into piles, which were afterward removed. Their use was productive of a very thorough and speedy final clearing.

Two types of snow-melting machines were given careful trials during the past winter. Of these the one using coke as fuel proved unsatisfactory; but the naphtha-burning machine showed a fair efficiency in all three storms, and was able, in the last two, to clear a long city block in from eight to ten hours. The cost of running is given by the superintendent of the company controlling the machine as $10.15 per hour, which, from the reports of the department inspector in charge of the experiments, is believed to be a fair estimate. With some improvements added since the last storm, the company claims a cost of $8 or less per hour, and an efficiency of a cubic yard of snow per minute.

The actual average efficiency for the last two storms of the winter (the number of yards melted being gaged by the loads removed in carts from parallel streets) was a little over two thirds of a cubic yard per minute. Granting, with the improvements proposed, an efficiency of one yard per minute, or sixty yards per hour, at a cost per hour (actual running expense only) of $10, the melting-machine of this type would dispose of the snow at a cost per yard of 16⅔ cents. If a machine were run at this rate the complete twenty-four hours without a breakdown, it would be equivalent to about thirty single carts, working both day and night, with a change of horses.

During the past winter the actual cost of carting per yard (exclusive of the shoveling items, piling and loading) was 25 cents. This would probably be increased to 30 cents, including the omitted items and taking into account the expense of manning and caring for the dumps. Considering the items of supervision identical in both cases, the showing, therefore, is in favor of the machine.

H. L. S.

CHAPTER XII

STREET-RAILROADS AND PAVEMENTS IN NEW YORK *

THE greatest single difficulty with which the Department of Street-Cleaning has to contend is that caused by the horrible condition of the railway-tracks in their relation to the pavement adjoining them. It is this consideration which first attracted my attention to the subject; but all who drive or ride the bicycle in the city streets must have had their attention called to the subject by their own unpleasant experiences.

This subject had forced itself on my attention in a general way, but had been tacitly accepted as inevitable. It was said perhaps very properly that the railway companies had laid their tracks according to some sort of agreement with the city, and that they could not be required to go to the expense of relaying them. It was not until I drove in Vienna that the full enormity of the situation in New York occurred to me. The railway-track there is substantially the same as that in use in a portion of First Avenue, recently laid under the direction

* Reprinted from "Harper's Weekly."

of General Collis. It is shown in Fig. 1. The rail is equally high on both sides of the flange-groove. This groove is not such as to catch a wheel. The rail is laid at the exact level of the pavement, so that one can drive across it at any angle without noticing it. There is no depression on either side of the rail to hold street dirt

FIG. 1.

or to make sweeping difficult. In Vienna, and in other European towns, rails of this character are kept clean by the railway companies. I saw two men, each with a suitable scraper-scoop, running along these grooves at an ordinary walking gait. A wheelbarrow, driven by another man between them, received the contents of their scoops. At the rate at which they were working, they

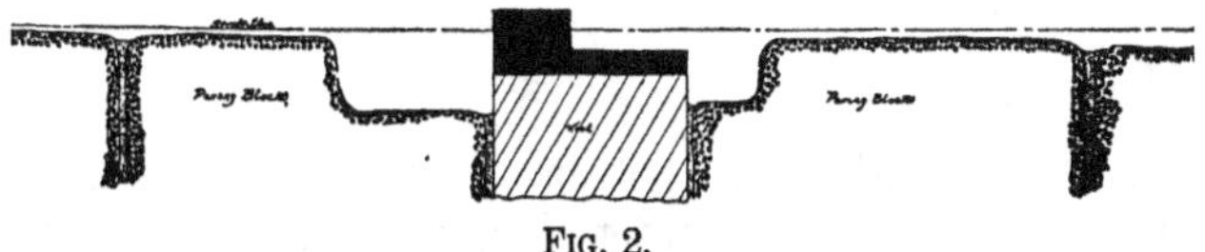

FIG. 2.

were cleaning at least two and a half miles an hour. This seems to me to be as near an approach to civilization in the matter of car-track and street pavement as we are likely to get, and it is near enough.

Now let us consider what we have to contend with. Fig. 2 shows the cross-section of pavement and rail opposite 15 Montgomery Street. There is a pocket for street dirt on both sides of the rail, and a serious obstruction to wagon traffic and wheeling is caused by the unyielding angular ridge of iron, standing higher than the street-line and much higher than the depression worn by traffic on both sides of the rail. When water accumulates in these depressions, there being generally a little play between the iron rail and the wood to which it is spiked, every time the rail is struck by a vehicle or depressed by the car-wheel there is apt to be a squirting of black juice over the clothing of the unfortunates who have not learned to keep a sharp eye out when they encounter such a condition.

Fig. 3, opposite 222 West Fourteenth Street, is different, but not better. The car-track seems here to have

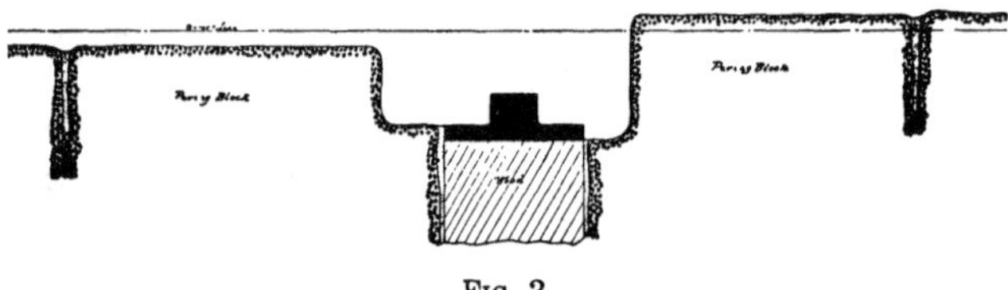

FIG. 3.

retired modestly to the bottom of its hole, but the power for mischief and discomfort is quite as great as in the other case.

Even worse is the condition shown in Fig. 4, opposite 312 Canal Street. The drop from the top of the pavement to the bottom of the pocket in this case is eight inches. This cavern has been worked out by heavy trucks, and is so conspicuous that it is avoided by lighter vehicles as the edge of a precipice would be, and in so far is less annoying to those who care what kind of street it is over which they drive. But imagine what a problem it offers to the poor "white angel" whose office it is to keep this cañon clean!

Opposite 423 Canal Street we have the pleasing combination shown in Fig. 5.

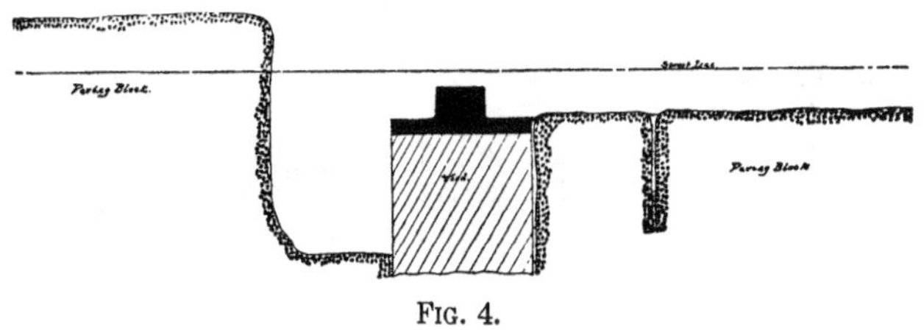

FIG. 4.

Fig. 6, opposite 160 West Fourteenth Street, shows another similar combination.

And these are fully matched at 23 Center Street (Fig. 7), within a stone's throw of the city hall.

Opposite 19 West Houston Street (Fig. 8) the difficulty is different, but not less. The narrow slot between the

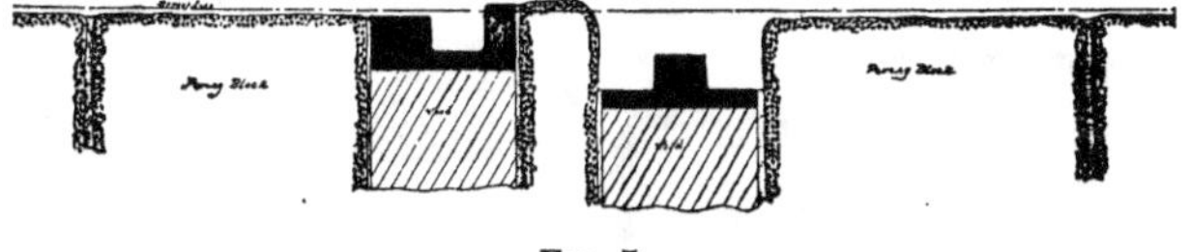

FIG. 5.

paving-stone and the rail is too narrow for a sweeper's broom, and it is narrow enough to grip a buggy-wheel with fatal effect.

Fig. 9 shows the condition of the Third Avenue track at Twenty-ninth Street. Comment is unnecessary; "it beggars description."

These illustrations are selected from a large number

that have been measured and platted, with a view to calling the attention of the different railway companies and of the Department of Public Works to the subject. Others would be given did space suffice, but surely these are enough to elicit the attention of the public; and the

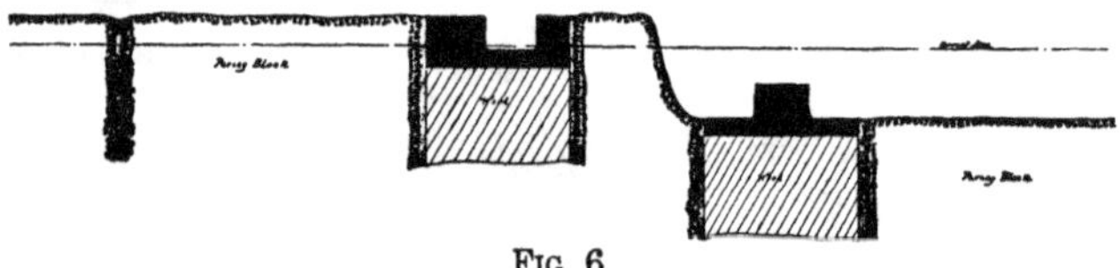

FIG. 6.

parallel of the conditions shown may be observed in all parts of the city where old tracks are in use.

It is not worth while here to go into the theory as to the manner in which these excavations have been caused by these tracks. It is all clearly explainable and easily understood. The important fact is that the conditions exist, and that the city cannot afford to allow them to

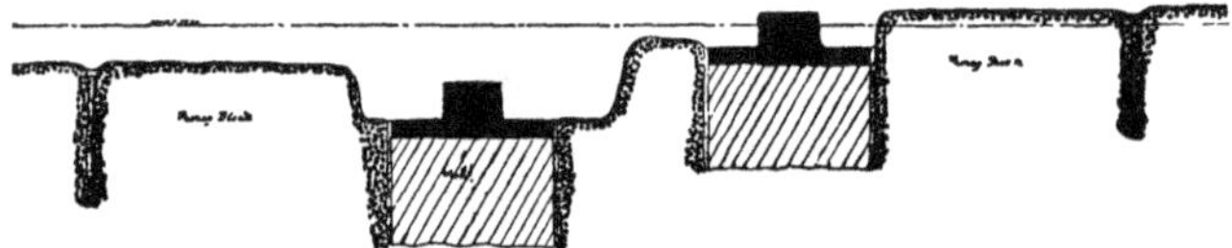

FIG. 7.

continue. Consider the great strain put upon all vehicles coming in contact with such holes and humps as are shown, the serious straining and permanent injury of horses due to the sudden dropping of a wheel into one of these pits, and the breaking of harness; and then consider what a saving it would be to the people, in the matter of dollars and cents, if all of these defective conditions were obliterated and all rail and adjoining pavement were brought into the condition shown in Fig. 1. Consider too—and this is a more serious matter than would at first appear—the amount of profanity and bad temper that the universal dissemination of similar conditions is fostering and developing throughout the whole driving section of the population. These are important

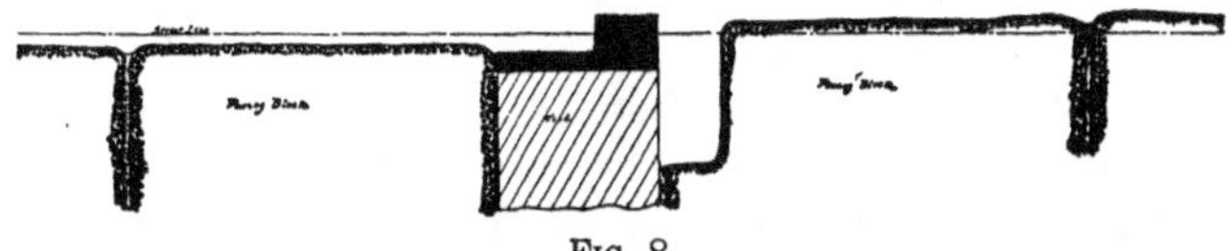

FIG. 8.

considerations, and are of themselves enough to warrant the cost of a radical reform; but it is not chiefly these that move me to make an appeal to public sentiment to exert itself in the matter. The reporters, with their invariable certainty of error, have quoted me on several occasions as saying that if the proper relation between

FIG. 9.

car-track and pavement could be established the $1,200,000 now spent for sweeping might be reduced to $700,000. Of course I never said anything of the kind. What I did say was that if we could secure this condition, and, in addition thereto, could have all of the streets of suitable grade paved with asphalt, then we could save this $500,000 a year. The saving from the mere improvement of car-track conditions would be much greater than would be supposed by those who have not watched the efforts and the various devices of the sweepers to get their accumulated dirt across one of these tracks, or to clear out the cavities formed beside them.

The subject need not be enlarged upon; it speaks for itself; and I say no more about it, for fear of occupying space that ought to be devoted to the illustrations, further than to make the remark that if the railway companies cannot be made to remedy the difficulty themselves, —and perhaps they cannot be,—the city could well afford, with a view to the saving that would result in the matter of street-sweeping alone, to make these changes at its own expense. Many of the horse roads are about to be changed to power roads. In all such cases new tracks must be laid, and it is within the power of the Department of Public Works to control both track and pavement, as has been done in First Avenue. These roads being eliminated, the cost of correcting those that may remain will be relatively unimportant. Their correction is imperative.

CHAPTER XIII

STREET-CLEANING IN EUROPE: A REPORT OF OBSERVATIONS MADE IN THE SUMMER OF 1896

VIENNA

THE impression produced by the streets of Vienna on the newly arrived American is altogether favorable. The pavement is much more uniformly good than he sees at home. There is less asphalt than we have, but the granite blocks, which are almost universal, are very regular and are very closely laid. They are perfect cubes of about eight-inch size; their surfaces are flat and their edges are sharp. As they are stacked in the depot, a dozen rows high and in piles some fifty feet long, they lie almost as close and true to line as so many pressed bricks. In the streets they are laid, on a true foundation of concrete, in diagonal rows, the lines of their opposite corners running straight across from curb to curb. The surface is as nearly flat as the need for drainage will allow—much flatter than with us. I should say that on a roadway twenty-five feet wide the middle is not more than two inches higher than the edge, and there is no perceptible deviation from a true surface either crosswise or lengthwise of the street. The joints between the blocks do not average more than a quarter of an inch. The material is hard, but it seems not to become slippery after years of use. The asphalt pavement is equally good, and both are on the average decidedly better than with us. The curbstones are heavier and lower, and the sidewalks are very carefully laid—often with the same blocks as the streets.

The tracks of the street-railroads are grooved rails, somewhat like those on Broadway, but they are heavier, and the two sides of the rail are equally high and equally broad. The groove in which the flange of the wheel runs is narrower than the narrowest carriage-wheel, so that, in driving, the wheel passes obliquely to and fro over the track without interference from it or from the pavement beside it. Contrasted with our "center-bearing rail," with a deep wide groove between it and the stone on each side of it, angering the driver, wrenching the vehicle and shortening its life, this Viennese device is most attractive. From the street-cleaner's point of view, the small channel (to be cleaned by the railway-man's scraper) is a vast gain over the two deep wide ruts that no broom can clean properly. Doubtless the cost of introducing this improved rail in New York would be covered in a very short time by the saving of wear and tear of vehicles and harness, and by the greater durability of the adjacent pavement, to say nothing of the comfort and cleanliness which it is one of the first duties of city government to secure. As an incident of the changing of motive-power and other work, a number of tracks are now receiving the new rail.

The sidewalks are uniformly and always clean; they are swept twice a day by the householders, and, except in the colder months, they are sprinkled twice a day by some domestic device, ranging from a large bottle, or a pail of water and a whisk, to a watering-can. I asked the head of the street-cleaning service if he had difficulty in securing the proper performance of this work. He said that he gave it no attention whatever; that all the people do it as a matter of course, just as they attend to the floors of their houses, especially to those which may be seen by others. I frequently saw persons turn aside to spit in the street; I never saw one spit on the sidewalk. I mention these deviations from the cherished practices of my native land not because I am "un-American," but because it was my purpose to learn what I could and to report what I learned.

In the matter of street-sweeping we are at no such disadvantage. Our best-paved streets, though not so well paved as these, are better cleaned; and our worst streets, with a pavement that would not be tolerated anywhere in Europe, are cleaner than the average of all except the best in Vienna. The finer thoroughfares in the central part of the city are swept by machine between eleven and four in the night—so much as can be done by ten two-horse machines with their attendant sprinkling-carts. I drove out at four o'clock, but was already too late to overtake them at their work. In some places I found the sweepers taking up the "stroke" of the machines. It was trifling in amount, because these streets are constantly swept in the daytime. The machines give a fair start in the morning; but this is a very busy town, and when the men came on for their work at six there was already much for them to do.

The sweeping force cannot compare with our own. Many of the men are old, few of them seem to be industrious, and they dress like the New York sweepers of days long past. They use long-handled birch-brooms, which they swing over a wide swath, and when the street is dry they raise a merry cloud of dust. Some of them used (and most of them seemed to have) cans with very long spouts terminating in rose-sprinklers. The can is held against the breast, and the body is swayed from side to side, throwing the water over a considerable width. It seemed a good plan. Aside from the broom and can, each sweeper has a shovel, an odd-shaped dust-pan, and a medieval two-wheeled hand-cart, weighing as much as a buggy.

The dust-pan has a sheet-iron bottom about eighteen inches square, and wooden sides and back about eight inches high (the back higher than the sides). From the back there rises vertically a handle of narrow board, with a hole for the hand; the board reaches to about the height of the armpit. This is held with the left hand and arm, the iron bottom flat on the ground, and the long broom is worked with the right hand. When the pan is full it is carried to the side of the street and dumped in small piles. In due time the hand-cart is trundled to one pile after another and is filled with the shovel. Then it is wheeled away to some convenient place where the traffic is not too active, and its contents are shoveled out and added to a fast-growing heap, which is afterward shoveled into the great wagons that haul it away to the point of final disposal.

Vienna is divided into nine wards. Only the first (*Bezirk I.*), the fine central part, is cleaned entirely by the city's own force. The others are largely cared for by contractors. There is a good deal of macadam in all the wards, even in the central one. The areas are recorded by square meters, which is necessary because some streets are 200 feet wide, and some not over 20 feet, with roadways in proportion. The whole roadway area is equal to about 550 miles of our streets. The paved street area of the first ward equals only about 25 miles of ours. This is all as well cleaned as the Bowery and Grand Street, much of it as well as Fifth Avenue and Broadway.

The cost of cleaning this 25 miles, including the removal of sweepings and house wastes, sprinkling twice a day in the warmer months, and removing all the snow in winter, is about 400,000 gulden. At the present rate of exchange the gulden is worth 41½ cents. In wages it is worth, as compared with street-cleaners' wages in New York, about $2.94. That is to say, the pay of a sweeper in Vienna is 1 gulden per day, and he works ten hours. Our men get $2.30, and they work not much more than eight hours. All expenses are in about the same proportion, and this is to be remembered when the cost of our work is compared with that of Europe. A mile of street in the heart of Vienna (calculated to our width) costs, sprinkling and snow included, about 16,000 gulden a year. A mile of average street in New York costs, without sprinkling and snow, $7190. As indicated above, our men work more faithfully, and our streets, on the average, are cleaner. The outlying eight wards in Vienna are mostly very imperfectly cleaned. The outlay for the whole city is only about 1,500,000 gulden.

The average cost of snow removal *in the first ward* is from 80,000 to 100,000 gulden. After heavy storms as many as 12,000 extra men are hired—mainly in the first ward—and thousands of teams are hired. A bargain is made with each to haul away the snow from a given area.

The work is well systematized as to all that is done by the department, save that the sweepers are not kept up to the mark as they might be. The chief overseer of each district gets only 1500 gulden per year, while our district superintendent gets $1800; but he is usually a man of good position. He esteems it a great honor to have such important work intrusted to him, and he devotes himself to it.

The collection of house wastes goes on all day, but the collecting-wagons have notice given of their coming, by bell or otherwise, and the garbage, etc., in boxes and baskets of every sort, are set out just in time for them. These wagons are very large and cumbersome, and they are covered. They collect sweepings and house wastes indiscriminately, and are hauled out about an hour's distance into the country, where their contents are turned over to the "scow-trimming" contractor of the locality. The unsalable refuse is finally used for filling depressions left by the old course of the Danube. The contractor and his wife work at the "picking" like the men, women, and children whom they employ. Their business is well managed, and little that can be turned to account is allowed to escape. An important item of their collection is fuel—bits of wood, cinders, coal, etc.; and this is made the subject of a very Yankee-like piece of cleverness. The workmen are allowed to carry home all of this material that they collect on Saturday. They seem not to consider that the sufficiency of their output in the same line on the other five days of the week is measured by the Saturday standard.

It is hardly necessary to say that no fair comparison

can be made between the street-cleaning work of this city and that of New York, even if it would be proper for me to make it. The conditions are all very different. Some of our methods could be adopted with advantage in Vienna, and some of their apparatus would be worth trying in New York. For example, their sweeping-machines are of a much better pattern than ours, and they have a snow-plow that is most useful. Though this latter costs about 900 gulden, the street-railways use 200 of them, and the city has nearly the same number for its own work.

There are street-sprinkling wagons of various sorts. One has about eight feet of hose leading from its tap, and a boy, walking at a safe distance behind it, jerks a connecting-rope in such a way as to swing the end of the hose from side to side, throwing a good spray over a width of four yards or more. This seems crude, but it is effective. Another wagon which finds much favor in the department is a very complete machine. Its reservoir of iron is hermetically sealed, and it has an air-pump, worked by the revolution of a hind wheel by means of a sprocket and chain (like a bicycle). The pressure may be regulated anywhere from one ounce to thirty pounds per square inch, and the spray may be delivered to the rear or to either side at will, or to the full half-circle. Everything is under the easy control of the driver. The work is effective for a width of twenty-five feet or more, or less, according to the pressure given. It is a great advantage of this watering-wagon that it sprinkles the streets without deluging them.

BUDAPEST

Budapest, although it is now celebrating its thousandth anniversary, is practically a new city. To those who are fond of international comparisons, it is "the Chicago of Europe." The comparison is not altogether apt, for Budapest is very well and handsomely built to its outer edges, and its public buildings and public places are regal in their aspect, while it has very little of the wonderful industrial and business activity of Chicago. Its principal streets are wide and long, and they have stretched out over the level plain with marvelous rapidity. Both towns have grown too fast, and are now feeling the effect in the form of financial lassitude. Here the resemblance stops.

From the point of view of the street-cleaner, no comparison is possible, for the Hungarian capital is very clean. It is—save in some of its older streets—unusually well paved where it is paved, and perfectly macadamized where it is not paved. Andrassystrasse, the finest and longest street, is paved with wood, after the best London and Paris model—than which, when it is well kept, nothing in the world is better, from the street-cleaning point of view.

In the matter of the sweeping of streets and sidewalks and of the collection of household wastes, the methods here are substantially the same as in Vienna, save that the sweepers are active young men and are much more industrious. Other differences are only in details of little importance, except with regard to the cab-stands, which are many and are actively used. These are generally a little lower than the street, are graded to a sewer inlet, and are asphalted. They are swept and thoroughly flushed and scrubbed several times a day, so that the usual odor and untidiness of such places are entirely obviated.

The area of paved streets is equal to about 150 miles of New York streets. The cost of snow removal in the winter of 1895–96 was 160,000 gulden. Wages are 1 gulden per day. The entire cost for all cleaning, snow removal, transportation of wastes, and street-sprinkling averages about 800,000 gulden per year.

In the matter of final disposition Budapest is very instructive and interesting. Everything is hauled to a station some three miles away. Here the wagons, night-soil vans, etc., are dumped into cars standing in a tunnel under the dumping-platforms. The loaded trains run out about three miles farther, to Kleinpest, a point remote from all population, save for the two hundred and fifty men, women, and children working about the disposal plant. They are a curious community. The works have been in operation for some thirty years, and most of those now employed were born in the "Kehrichtring" (Rubbish Boulevard), as they call their village. They are not an attractive community, and the older members are said to spend most of their wages in drink. Save for the effects of this dissipation, there is little sickness, and it is evidently not in itself an unhealthy industry in which they are engaged.

The whole business of final disposition is in the hands of a contractor who has controlled it for twenty years or more. He is a very wealthy man and a large landholder, whose interest lies largely in the value of the manure for his farms. He owns the dump, the railroad and its equipment, and the separating machinery. He receives from the city 115,000 gulden per year, in addition to the material delivered to him.

After this year his contract will be extended to include the collection in the town and the hauling to the dump; and he is building a branch line to connect his works with the state railroads, to widen the market for his fertilizers. He has, up to this time, made no money profit, but he has had a good supply of manure for home use, and has accumulated enormous deposits, which the new railroad connection will enable him to sell.

The separation-works were started nearly thirty years ago by Mr. Ignatius Fischer, who was then the contractor. He had more ingenuity and enterprise than capital, and he became the manager of the works under his successor. He is a man of quick intelligence, and has built up, little by little, with the aid of a competent mechanical engineer and lately of a chemist, a very complete factory for the separation of the wastes and the manufacture of fertilizers, etc. The chemist was for some years with Edison in New York. He is now carrying on successful experiments in the direction of the development of ammonia and other marketable products from certain parts of the refuse. Nearly all of the handling and separation of the material is done by machinery, only the culling out of the salable wastes requiring manual labor.

The apparatus is contained in a large four-story brick building with ample steam-power, unsalable rubbish being the fuel used. The railroad-cars are unloaded into small tram-wagons, which are hauled by an endless chain from a tunnel under the track up a steep slope to the top of the building, where they are dumped into the mouth of a coarse revolving screen, which holds back large sticks, boxes, old baskets, broken watermelons (this is the land of the best and cheapest watermelons in the world), and other large objects. What passes through the wide meshes of this screen runs into another with a very close mesh. This takes out the dust and the fine horse-manure as ground up by the wheels and the sweepers in the streets, and sends it to the wagons running to the manure-dumps. The next screen divides the remaining material roughly into two grades, for easier hand-picking.

The picking-tables, which are very long, are furnished with endless aprons of heavy hemp cloth about two feet wide. These move slowly between two rows of women and children, who select the various treasures to which they are assigned, each after its kind. The white-bottle boy lets the green bottles pass, and the big-bone woman pays no attention to the small bones; these meet their fate farther on. One group of children devotes itself entirely to corks, another to nails, another to strings, and so on. As the cloth finally turns over the end of the table it drops all of its rejected material into a conveyer, which carries it to the manure-wagon. In the heap to which it is added there goes on a process of "bacteriolysis" that reduces it all to the condition of a fine compost fit for the fields. Curiously (to us), no use is made of paper or rags, save as they are required for fuel. The wood-pulp industry and the German tariff on paper stock have robbed them of all commercial value. This, too, in the face of a minuteness of economy that is careful not to let a single old cork escape, although the only sale for the corks is to make fenders for the use of the boats on the Danube. Nothing that has the slightest selling value is allowed to escape, and what cannot be sold in its present form is turned over to the productive industry of the microbes of the compost-heaps.

It seemed to me that these very complete works, developed through years of patient study of the refuse of the saving population of Budapest, presented food for much thought to one whose official functions compel him to dump outside of Sandy Hook two and a half million cubic yards a year of the wastes of the wasteful city of New York, where rags and paper sell for a good price. Our conditions are very different from those of Budapest, and different measures must be taken here; but if we can ever reach the minute economy of the works at Kleinpest, we ought, with our richer refuse and our higher prices, to derive an income from our rubbish sufficient to pay much of the cost of running the Department of Street-Cleaning. In support of this opinion it is to be said that the recovery and sale of paper, rags, bottles, metals, rubber, wood, coal, bone, grease, corks, strings, shoes, hats, and other things that are thrown away, to the value of half a cent a day for each member of the population, should that be possible, would amount to much more than the whole appropriation for street-cleaning. We may never reach this figure, but the sum total thus to be saved will surely be very large, and the experience of Budapest is full of promise and instruction for us.

BERLIN

For several reasons Berlin offers special attractions as a field for the study of street-cleaning methods from the point of view of the work in New York. In the first place, it is the only large city in Europe in which the sweepers are uniformed—beyond a special cap or badge, serving for identification, but not modifying the variegated clothing of the common workman. In the next place, Mr. Albert Shaw, in his "Municipal Government in Continental Europe," gives prominence to the cleanly condition of the streets, and he sets forth in detail and very clearly the excellent government of Berlin; while Miss Colbron's paper in the New York "Times" last spring indicated a very good management of the Department of Street-Cleaning.

My investigation showed almost at the outset the correctness of the Berlin department's own statement, in its last annual report, that "comparisons with other great cities cannot convey a correct impression as to the relative cost of the work, because the conditions are so different."

This applies to methods and to results as well as to cost. For example, in New York we sweep every street at least once a day; we do not sprinkle the streets; we do not sweep the sidewalks; we remove all household refuse; and we are charged with the final disposition of street and household wastes of every kind. This last item costs us about $475,000 per year. In Berlin, on the other hand, the department sweeps the streets on an average of only three times a week; it sprinkles the streets; it sweeps all the sidewalks; it has nothing whatever to do with household wastes of any kind, neither ashes, garbage, nor refuse; it disposes only of the dirt swept up in the streets and from the sidewalks, and it pays a contractor for this removal only about $140,000.

With us practically no street dirt is allowed to be run into the sewers. In Berlin all that can be made liquid enough is so disposed of. We have to find our own points of disposal,—thus far at sea,—while in Berlin this is the lookout of the contractor.

It is clear, therefore, that, however much we may find that is of interest, we cannot make useful comparisons as to cost nor as to processes. The rate of wages and the number of persons employed differ in a most important degree. Our force numbers about 2700, of all grades, and we pay our sweepers and drivers an average of about $680 per year. In Berlin the force numbers only about 900, men and boys, and their average pay is not more than about $260 per year. Our annual outlay is about $3,000,000; that of Berlin is about $760,000. The two cities are of very nearly the same population.

Therefore, setting comparison aside, let us see just what the work of the department is in Berlin, and how it is done.

The more frequented streets are swept every day, others three times a week, others twice a week, and others again only once a week. Those that are not swept daily are looked to pretty constantly, and any excessive fouling is removed by ambulant gangs employed for this purpose. The sidewalks are swept early in the morning. Very much of the street-sweeping is done by machinery, by contractors, and this is almost exclusively night-work, beginning at eleven o'clock and ending before six in the morning. The "stroke" of the machine is swept into heaps, shoveled into wheelbarrows, and dumped at convenient points, from which it is taken by the contractors' wagons. I was out on one very rainy night and found a good deal of this dirt being run into the sewer inlets. In these much of the sand is held back by a trap, while much sand and most of the mud enter the sewers, from which it is necessary from time to time to remove deposits by flushing or by mechanical means.

As in all European cities, sand is used very freely to prevent the slipping of horses on the pavements, especially on asphalt and wood. The sanding and the removal of the ground-up sand add much to the work of the department.

The asphalt pavement is mainly very good. The same can hardly be said for the wood pavement. And this is evidently the universal opinion of the cab-drivers. I had no opportunity to inquire into the reason for this defect, which does not exist in London and Paris, but I was especially struck with the fact that a wide expanse of wood pavement on Unter den Linden, near the museum, was a series of small pools during rain, and that driving over this in any weather was very jolty business as compared with the asphalt in its neighborhood. Such irregularity of surface is a great drawback to successful machine-sweeping, and adds to the labor of hand-sweeping. Without noticeable exception, however, the pavement of this city is far, very far, from being so bad as that of most New York. It is only our asphalt streets that are as good as these. On the other hand, there are in Berlin many macadamized streets which get only a superficial cleaning.

The question of the pay and the general treatment of the men is well worth our consideration. As we have seen, the rate of wages is very low. A gang-leader gets only 93 cents per day; a workman of the first class only 81 cents; a workman of the second class only 68 cents; and a boy only 40 cents. These are more than the usual rate of wages, not only in Berlin, but in the country generally. From the standard of comfortable support, these amounts are obviously sufficient. The employees are strong, well fed, and in good condition, and the service is eagerly sought after; for, aside from the pay, the attending conditions are very favorable. In the first place, the city furnishes uniforms and tools, and it takes good care of its working-people. The boys, who are used mainly for cleaning the streets of horse-droppings and litter during the daytime, are taken on at the age of sixteen or seventeen. When they reach the age for military service they go into the army, and they have a preference for reëmployment after their discharge. The second-class men, who number only about seventy in all, are raised to the first class within a single year, and sometimes earlier when especial fitness for the work is shown. After four years of satisfactory service the men are assured their positions for life, with the pensions and other benefits provided for. In other words, employment in the street-cleaning service opens a life-career to those who properly fulfil the requirements of their positions.

The work is exacting rather than hard. The regular men who follow the sweeping-machines work from midnight until eight in the morning; but they have a half-hour for breakfast, so that their actual work is only for seven and a half hours. The day men work from seven in the morning till seven in the evening in summer, and from eight till eight in the winter; but they have three hours for breakfast, dinner, and supper, making the time of actual working nine hours per day. The force is changed about so that each has his fair share of day and night work. On Sundays and holidays the day men work only from six to nine in the morning, and they receive full pay for these days.

At the same time they are considered to be on duty every day at all hours, so that in the case of floods, heavy storms, snow, etc., they may be called on at any time for any amount of extra work. They are legally entitled to no extra pay for this; but the department has a small fund, furnished by the City Council, from which it may, and does, in its discretion, give a gratuity to those who have done especially well, or who may have shown special efficiency or fidelity in their work. This is accepted gratefully as a bonus, not received as a right. Taking the year through, day and night,—Sundays, holidays, and all,—and counting emergencies, the work averages eight hours per day.

One of the best features of the system is the manner in which illness and disability are treated. If a man is disqualified by sickness he is paid his full wages for three days. After that his pay ceases, but he gets the benefit of the sick-fund. If he is permanently disabled, supposing him to be a life-member of the force, the City Council awards him, in addition to the benefits to which he is entitled from the sick-fund, etc., from $100 to $150 per year for the rest of his life. If he is able to do light work, light work he must do; but if he has been for four years a faithful member of the street-cleaning force, he is sure of support till he dies. It is to be remembered that in Berlin soul and body can be comfortably kept together for even as little as $100 per year.

The gratuity from the Council comes from a fund of $1000, which has been maintained, since before the establishment of the sick-fund, for use in the relief of special cases. From this source a disabled man may receive an amount equal to one half his regular wages; and it sometimes happens that with this and the sick-fund—especially when a man is entitled to draw from two such funds—an idle man gets more than a workingman's pay. Such instances are very exceptional. As a rule, men who have been in receipt of benefits are very glad to get back to work again.

The sick-fund was established in 1892, but in this short time it has proved to be a great benefit, and the results have been most satisfactory. In 1894, out of a membership of 900, 318 received more or less help from the fund. The receipts of the fund were $8462, and the payments for disability were $4975. At the end of 1894 the invested fund amounted to $7281. The prosperity was such that the committee was directed at the general meeting to increase the benefit from half-pay for thirteen weeks' sickness to two-thirds pay for twenty-six weeks, and the death payment was raised from twenty days' pay to forty days' pay. Unmarried men in hospitals receive one tenth of the amount of their wages for pocket-money. The flourishing condition of the fund makes these liberal disbursements safe. In addition to this fund, there is a voluntary funeral fund, which gives aid to the families of deceased members.

In addition to all this, men who have served for twenty-five years get special extra compensation. In short, everything possible is done to make each individual man feel that he is not so much an employee of the department as one of its members, and that for the rest of his life he is sure of care, protection, and support.

The uniform is modest and neat rather than conspicuous, and is thus less useful in calling public attention to the care the streets are receiving and in enlisting public aid in the avoidance of littering. Perhaps it is better suited to the temper of the people of Berlin; but it cannot be doubted that in New York the fact that the sweepers stare the public in the face in every street has had much effect in securing popular approbation and assistance. The belted blouse of the Berlin uniform is originally black, but the weather soon gives it a not unpleasant greenish hue; the cap is flat and not large; and the trousers, at this season at least, are of unbleached duck—both long, for good weather, and short, with long boots, for rainy days. Some of the men and many of the boys have a black haversack strapped over the shoulder, in which are carried a water-proof cape, a hunk of black bread, etc.

As already indicated, all manner of household wastes are removed by private contractors, of whom there are some two hundred, large and small. They take these wastes from the interior of the house, and our unsightly "receptacles" and ash-barrels are never seen on the sidewalk. There is no systematic method of disposal. Those who remove house wastes, as well as those who haul away the street-sweepings, must provide their own dumping-places. Much is sold for manure, some is used for filling low lands, and some is deposited in useless heaps. The city is growing so rapidly that its refuse must be carried farther and farther afield, with an attendant increase of cost.

As a relief from this condition, very careful experiments have been carried on for a year or more in the direction of destruction by fire; but they have been abandoned because of the high cost of cremation when applied to Berlin refuse. While this process is reasonably economical in Hamburg, where English coal is largely used for fuel, leaving a certain amount of combustible cinder in the ash, which helps the burning, it is found that the "brown coal" and "briquettes" used in Berlin make much more ash, which has no remnant of fuel left in it. What is to be done in the matter is not yet determined.

I was not in the city long enough to form a correct opinion as to its cleanliness, and it rained much of the time, the rain helping the work in some ways and hindering it in others. I got the impression that it is not cleaner nor, save as to ash-barrels, more tidy than New York. Possibly longer observation, in better weather, would have given another impression.

PARIS

It was with especial interest that I made my first examination of the streets of Paris, for I remembered them as being in excellent condition in 1889 (Exposition year).

After a close and careful examination, I should say that they are quite as well swept as our streets, and that there is nowhere to be found the defective pavement of which we have so much. In the matter of litter, however, I think that New York is much better cared for. Except in the more frequented show streets, and to a certain extent even there, there is more paper scattered, and in many parts of the town much less attention seems to be paid to its collection and removal. On the whole, I think we lose nothing in the comparison. New York is as clean and at least as tidy as Paris. The methods of work in the French capital are in many respects different from what was found in other cities, and very different from the methods here.

In 1859 the cleaning of the streets was transferred from the Préfecture de Police to the Préfecture de la Seine, and it was then placed in the hands of the Engineering Department. The cost at that time could not be learned; but the cost in 1872 was 3,808,000 francs; in 1877 it was 4,618,000; in 1889 it was 6,530,000. It is now about 8,000,000 francs. Formerly it was the duty of all property-owners to clean one half of the street, if this did not exceed 6 meters (20 feet). This work is now done by the city, and is paid for by a special tax on the property, which, for this purpose, is divided into three classes: that occupied (1) by buildings, (2) by walls or open grounds, (3) by vacant lots. In no case is the charge more than the actual cost to the city; in some cases it is materially less. Property-holders must still remove snow and ice from the sidewalks, according to specific regulations.

The total surface swept (1889) was 15,562,000 square meters. Of this, the property taxed paid for 8,721,000 meters, and the city for 6,840,000. The amount of the tax was 3,140,000 francs. The average cost per square meter was 36 centimes (7 cents) per annum.

The sweeping force is divided into 149 gangs. In the central part of the city each gang consists of a foreman, assistant foreman, and 20 to 25 men or women, most of whom work during the morning at the necessary sweeping and assist in the loading of the wagons. In the afternoon only the regular route men are at work. They keep the streets in order, wash the gutters and urinals, care for markets, etc. Outside of the center, the gangs consist of 1 foreman, 4 route men, and 15 to 20 sweepers, the last usually working only in the forenoon. Work begins at 4 A. M. all the year round. The half-day ends at 11 A. M., and the full day at 4 P. M. The entire force consists of 3200 regular hands, with extra men for emergencies. The pay is by the hour, the men receiving 32, 34, and 37 centimes, and the women, children, and old men, 25, 27, and 30 centimes. The route men are paid by the month—120 to 125 francs for the leaders, and 105 francs for the ordinary men. Of this they are required to pay 5 francs per month into a savings fund, which is repaid to them when they quit the service. All men regularly employed are also obliged to join a mutual benefit society.

The workmen of the street-cleaning service of Paris are not uniformed, and, except for their numbered badges, they are not to be distinguished from other working-men. The slouchy and often faded blue or black blouse so generally worn is neither distinctive nor attractive. It is comfortable, cheap, and cheap-looking.

Sweeping-machines are used for auxiliary work on paved streets, and for emergencies, as during a thaw, and when it is required that the streets should be cleaned rapidly for special occasions.

All street-sprinkling is done by the city and under the direction of the engineers having charge of the cleaning. Sprinkling costs just about twice as much per square meter for macadam, of which there is a great deal, as for pavement. The water-carts weigh when empty about 1400 pounds, and when full about 4000 pounds, with the driver. Where water is conveniently furnished they deliver at least two loads per hour. The sprinklers cover a width of about 16 feet, and one load suffices for 800 to 900 square meters; 370 water-carts are now used. These belong to the city, which hires horses—one to each cart—and drivers at 340 francs ($68) per month.

More recently, on the principal streets, much use is made of jointed pipes attached to hydrant-cocks provided for the purpose. This apparatus is made of from 4 to 6 pieces of pipe, each 2 meters long, with flexible joints, and running on small, caster-like trucks. They reach to about 75 feet, and the cocks supplying them are about 150 feet apart. The work is very effective, and costs only half that of water-cart work.

On asphalt and wood much use is made of the squeegee (a rubber scraper). A man working this walks at least at the rate of two miles per hour and covers 1200 square meters. If strong and skilful he may cover 2000 meters. There is still a good deal of work done in a much more primitive and antiquated way. Water is set running in the gutters, and is dammed here and there by a bunch of untidy-looking old rags. The workman throws this water with a common scoop over the sidewalk and into the street. This does very well for washing sidewalks in conjunction with the squeegee, but its use is certainly not to be commended on the score either of tidiness or of economy. All pavements are sprinkled before sweeping if the weather is dry. If the streets are slimy from light rains the squeegee is used. Unless there is much mud or horse-manure, machines are not needed. When the machine is used, in wet weather or in dry, the stroke is gathered together with a common birch broom such as is used in Budapest and almost universally in European towns. The sweeping-machines used cover 6000 square meters per hour.

It is stated in the official report that what cannot be taken up is washed into the sewers, and that where there is much sand they save what they can of it for resanding the streets when slippery. To the ordinary observer it seems that they wash into the sewers all that can be got rid of in that way, and the accounts given of the amount of deposit regularly cleaned from the sewers would indicate that this method is carried to excess. It leads to the conclusion, which my earlier observation in other directions has indicated to be correct, that the sewers of Paris are many of them as dirty as the streets are clean.

In dry weather wood pavements are washed daily, asphalt every two days, and stone and macadam every three days. This washing is done between 4 and 8 A. M.

The order of work is as follows: From 4 to 6:30 A. M., sweeping and washing of sidewalks and streets, washing and disinfecting places soiled by urine, and cleaning public urinals; 6:30 to 8:30, assisting the wagons in taking up house wastes and general sweepings; 8:30 to 11, gathering droppings, washing gutters, sprinkling streets, cleaning and disinfecting urinals; 11 to 1, midday meal. This may be advanced to 10 o'clock, or put off till 12, if the exigencies of the work require it. Sometimes only one hour is allowed for the meal. In very hot weather the sprinkling is continued through this noon rest, the men taking turns, but each being allowed one hour for his repast. From 1 to 4 the same work as from 8:30 to 11; from 4 to 7 this work is continued in case of necessity; from 7 to 9 P. M., during the five winter months, continuing the occasional sanding of asphalt and wood which has gone on during the day. This is supplemental work, and the men do it by turns. The work about the markets continues from 7 A. M. to 9 P. M., at intervals, and as it can be done without interfering with the operations of the market-men. It includes the disinfection of all places soiled, as by cleaning fish, etc.

The official report of public works says: "The streets are sanded as many times during the day as is necessary to prevent the surface from becoming slippery. This is one of the operations of which the performance should never be delayed."

The garbage and other household refuse, as well as the sweepings of the streets, are taken up by the wagons between 6 and 8:30 A. M. in summer and between 7 and 9 in winter. Garbage was formerly placed at the edge of the sidewalks. This led to a very untidy condition from the scattering of the material by rag-pickers and others, and accidents resulted from the falling of broken bottles, pottery, etc., into the streets. To avoid this, owners are now obliged to provide for their tenants, from 9 P. M. until morning, one or more receptacles for all household wastes. These are set out at least an hour before the time for collection, and are taken in immediately after collection. They have to be kept in a sound and cleanly condition, and they can receive nothing but household wastes.

Every three years bids are received for the work of collection, the contractor becoming the owner of all that he collects. Formerly this resulted in a profit to the city—that is, the material was worth more than the cost of removal. Then for a time the value was about equal to the cost. At present the city pays for its removal over 2,000,000 francs per annum. One reason for this change of condition is that there is now a smaller number of subcontractors, such as the market-gardeners, who used to occupy lands now covered with buildings, and who aided the city contractors in their work and paid something for what they collected; another is the greater distance to which it is necessary to cart all refuse, because of the growth of the city, and especially because the authorities of suburban districts have become more severe in their requirements as to the deposit of waste materials. These conditions have also led to an increased cost of the material as delivered to farmers, so that these now prefer to buy stable manure. For purposes of removal the city is divided into sections, for which special rates of payment are tabulated. Selected and well-known contractors bid for each section—so much more or less than the fixed tariff. They are required to take all refuse from houses, restaurants, barracks, etc., to remove street-sweepings, including fallen leaves, all market refuse, and such spoiled food-supplies as are seized for bad condition. The contractor himself chooses the route for the working of the different wagons in his section, but this is subject to the control of the engineer, with a view to the prevention of overloading, interference with traffic, and too early hours for the comfort of people who are not early astir. These routes cannot be changed without the approval of the authorities. In regulating them the contractor arranges for a certain amount of work to be done by farmers' wagons at convenient hours and places. The contractor's vehicles are generally large, with broad tires for country travel. They have a hoisting apparatus for loading, and are served by two men.

The coming of the wagon to remove household refuse is announced by the ringing of a specified bell. It is required that all wagons be kept painted and thoroughly disinfected, and the administration has control over the men as well as the vehicles. The city provides three men or women during the two hours of collection to assist in loading each wagon. If receptacles are roughly handled and injured, the employee is held responsible, and is obliged to pay for repairing or replacing them.

The contract for the removal of refuse includes an obligation to furnish teams for sweeping-machines and water-carts at a fixed tariff. In case of need, the contractor must help in the removal of snow and ice. The contractor must present himself daily, at a fixed hour, at the engineer's office for instructions, and he is obliged to keep his own office open from 8 A. M. to 4 P. M. and to maintain telephonic connection there.

A two-horse-wagon service, including the collection of house wastes and sweepings,—that is, including everything that is to be carted away,—serves an average population of about 3500. Each wagon costs the city, on an average, from 10 to 11 francs per day.

No comparison can be made as to the cost of carting in Paris and New York. The French are less wasteful than we are, and household refuse consequently amounts to less; but, on the other hand, we have to remove everything, while a very large part of the street-sweepings of Paris is run into the sewers.

There is one curious thing about the collection of the materials in Paris: that is, that the rag-pickers seem to be under the special protection of the government, and are allowed full swing at the receptacles as they stand on the sidewalks, and even on the wagons as they are being loaded. What we call "scow-trimming," for which the city of New York receives a large sum, is thus abandoned to individual enterprise, and is carried on at the source of supply rather than at the point of dumping.

Efforts thus far made in Paris to utilize garbage have resulted in loss. It was thought that the shells of mussels and oysters might be converted into a manure; but this scheme has been given up, and they are now dumped into abandoned quarries in the vicinity of the city.

The question of distant transportation of the city's wastes, by water or by rail, has been carefully investigated, and the outlook is not promising. Water transportation means a difficulty from droughts, which may interfere with it for weeks together, from floods, which are often serious, and from the freezing of the waterways. This method is therefore unavailable, because it is not reliable for the daily use which is absolutely necessary. Delivery by rail has thus far been found too expensive. In order to reach lands poor enough to make matters of this kind of value, it would be necessary to go so far as to make the lowest possible rate of freight prohibitory. The question has been mooted of establishing a model farm for the city, on which to demonstrate the value of the wastes.

Incineration has also been considered; but it was found that the original investment for buildings and machinery would amount to 6,000,000 francs, and that there would be the embarrassment that, while the material is collected in two hours in the morning, economical working would require the incineration to be continued uninterruptedly day and night. The whole question is still open, and it is an extremely knotty one. Everything points to a steady and large increase of the cost of final disposition, whatever method may be resorted to.

Neither in street-cleaning, in the removal of household wastes, nor in final disposition did I find any suggestions which would be of use in New York, save as to the value of the salable refuse.

Until and including the winter of 1879–80 the removal of snow and ice was carried on according to regulations promulgated by the Préfet de la Seine, which determined the obligations of property-owners and of the administration. These are still in force, at least with regard to the duty of owners, who have to clear their sidewalks of snow, putting it into the street or in banks on the walk itself; to break the ice in the gutters; to spread sand, ashes, or cinders on frozen surfaces; and finally, in certain cases,—but only on the formal requisition of the administration,—to pile the snow of the street itself.

At the beginning of each winter printed notices are served on all owners, reminding them of their obligations. It is to be admitted, however, that their concurrence is secured only with difficulty; it is often necessary to call in the aid of the police, to bring many suits at law, and to enforce judgment in a great number of cases. This complicates the work of the administration when all its energies are needed for the work on the streets. It is especially prohibited to deposit on the public thoroughfare any snow from roofs or from inner courtyards. There is published each year a list of places to which this snow may be carried.

Up to the date named the administration provided for the clearing of the streets with the ordinary force of street-cleaners, supplemented by numerous auxiliary workmen, by the fifty wagons which the omnibus company is required by the terms of its franchise to furnish, and by the teams which the city has the right to exact from the contractors who remove street-sweepings and house wastes. As all these resources were insufficient, contracts were at the beginning of the season made with private persons to furnish a certain number of wagons by the day. The city had no apparatus useful for snow work other than its sweeping-machines. The use of salt had not yet been seriously tried.

This organization had nearly always sufficed, because in Paris snow seldom lasts more than a few days, and thaws rapidly. But the experience of 1879–80 demonstrated that when much snow fell and the cold continued the usual methods were absolutely ineffective. As a consequence, new regulations were made, which have worked well. These were:

1. The organization of the entire force early in the season by defined areas, so that the foremen and the men should know just what they were to do at the beginning of a storm, and so that, without waiting for further orders, they should betake themselves immediately to their posts.

2. Fixing the order of operations for removing snow from the streets according to their importance.

3. The use of mechanical aids to hasten the removal, and the application of salt to hasten the melting, of the snow.

4. Dumping the snow into the river and discharging it into sewers.

5. The extensive coöperation of private enterprise, by turning over to contractors a portion of the hand-work and of the carting.

In time of snow all of the personnel of the Street-Cleaning Department is employed for its removal. Each gang has its appointed rendezvous, its sand, its salt, and its prescribed place of discharge.

The streets are divided into three general categories: (1) wide streets, where the snow is piled in two rows, leaving a central space of from fifteen to twenty-five feet wide, provisionally; it is to be widened if time permits, either by piling the snow upon the sidewalks or by putting it all in one row; (2) narrow and crowded streets, from which the snow must be entirely removed; and (3) streets where it is to be piled in a single row to remain until it melts.

The sweeping-machines are provided with special

brooms,—prepared in advance,—which have steel wires mixed in with the ordinary piassava. These can be substituted very quickly for the common broom. This system has the great advantage that it allows the use of a machine which is known to all and which is made ready for snow work in a moment. An extra horse is required. A rude sort of snow-plow is used to make the first opening in the middle of the street.

The use of salt for melting the snow is carried to a considerable extent. Pure, fine salt for this purpose is delivered at the railway-stations at about six dollars per gross ton—the state and city taxes, which amount to thirty-two dollars, being remitted. It was first used on a large scale in 1880. It produces a dark-colored slush, with a temperature of about 10° F., which will not freeze unless the thermometer falls below this degree. When it does not interfere too much with traffic in the streets it is often left in place for several days, because it does not freeze and is to a considerable extent a preventive of slipping. If it becomes too thick it is removed with scrapers or with sweeping-machines. "Another property that is much appreciated in the use of salt in Paris is that it is the more rapid the more active the traffic; on streets of great travel the snow of the salted surface is reduced to mud in two hours."

The salt is spread from wheelbarrows by the shovel, and does not need to be very uniform. It is estimated that to melt packed snow to a depth of from one inch and a half to two inches about five ounces of salt are required per square yard. If the snow (packed) is six or eight inches deep, a surface layer is first melted and removed, and the lower layer is salted in turn. So far as the very complete official report is concerned, no account is taken of the effect of the salt-and-snow mixture on the health of the people, which is here thought to be serious.

From those parts of the city which are conveniently near the snow is dumped into the Seine, either at the landings or through openings in the parapet walls, which are closed after the winter weather is over. For remoter districts the sewer-openings are used as much as possible. Special snow-openings are made in the larger sewers. As much water as possible is run into them, and men standing on the banquettes of the sewers push the snow forward. There are used for the snow service 512 ordinary manholes and 121 special snow-openings.

As above stated, before 1880 the removal of snow was carried on by the city alone, with its own forces and thousands of workmen hired for the occasion. These it had to supply with tools, and it had to arrange for their regular and frequent payment. From lack of organization and discipline these men did slow work, and they were all the more ready to take advantage of the situation because they were working for the public. It was therefore determined, following the custom in other European cities, to let out portions of the work to contractors. The city was divided into sections, well regulated as to convenience of carting and dumping, and a price was fixed per cubic meter for loading and removal. The administration, with its own men and machines, piles the snow in rows, and the contractors cart it away. This division of the work has been very satisfactory, especially with regard to rapidity of handling.

In addition to the above, certain work beyond their contract obligations is done by the omnibus and tramway companies, the city furnishing them sweeping-machines and scrapers, which they operate with their own teams.

The order of work is as follows: If snow falls in the daytime, the workmen, without waiting for it to stop, use their brooms, shovels, and hand-scrapers to move it toward the sides of the streets and from sidewalks in front of public property. House-owners do the same for their walks, urged thereto by the authorities. In this way the effort is made immediately to clear a sufficient width for foot-passengers and for vehicles.

Efforts are especially concentrated on streets of the first importance. If at the time of beginning work the snow is as much as four inches deep, so that it cannot be moved by hand, then the sweeping-machines are used for the middle of the carriageway, and the snow is piled in rows by the men.

If the morning finds a depth of six or eight inches, the horse snow-plows (or side-scrapers) are used to open a width of from fifteen to twenty-five feet. These are followed by sweeping-machines. If these means do not suffice to bare the pavement, or when travel has packed the snow almost to the consistency of ice, it is heavily sanded or is treated with salt to melt it. Freedom of circulation being thus assured, the carting is begun, and the men are sent to clear the streets of the second class, and the snow is carted from them. If a thaw has not set in by this time, the streets of the third class are cleared in their turn.

As soon as a thaw begins, nearly all the contract carting is suspended, and the hydrants are opened; all the sweeping-machines are set at work, the slush is pushed toward the sewer inlets, "and in a short time the city has taken on its usual aspect."

The foregoing has been gleaned from the official reports of the "Directions of Works" of the Department of the

Seine. It is written after nearly two weeks' struggle with the very heavy and badly drifted snow of December 15, and when the banks and piles of snow in three quarters of the streets of New York are frozen solid. I have tried in vain to find a way in which the Paris prescription could have been made to give us relief.

LONDON

London is the most unsatisfactory town imaginable as a place in which to study municipal administration. It is an agglomeration of separate communities.

The "County Council," which controls the whole area in a general way and for some specific purposes, has no voice in the direction of local affairs, beyond establishing standards below which local work must not fall.

The "City" of London occupies a central area covering only one square mile in the heart of the town. It has a night population of only about 37,000, but its day population is about eight times as large, while more than a million persons enter it on every week-day, and its street traffic is enormous, nearly a hundred thousand carriages entering it daily. Surrounding this on all sides are some forty independent parishes and districts, each with its own local vestry or board, which directs all its local municipal affairs. The entire population of London is not far from five millions. There is no conspicuous dividing-line between the parishes; it is one great, solidly built town, with much uniformity of appearance. It is only when one attempts to study its methods of public work that its composite character appears.

The methods followed in the City are in a general way a type of the whole—varied in almost every case in minor details, to learn all of which would result in little valuable addition to common knowledge of street-cleaning operations. I shall therefore confine my remarks mainly to what is done in the City. The work here is under the control of the Commissioners of Sewers, whose engineer directs it. It includes street-cleaning, street-watering and washing, dusting, and removal of trade refuse. The force employed in 1896 consisted of 200 men, 180 boys, and 99 horses. There were used 79 vans, 16 water-wagons, with sweeping-machines, etc.

The arrangement of the work is as follows: All of the streets are swept daily, and in hot weather the main thoroughfares are squeegeed two or three times a day. The boys constituting the "street-orderly" system work on all the main streets and on some of the secondary ones. These active youngsters with their pans and brushes gather up the horse-droppings almost as they fall, emptying them into boxes fixed for the purpose at the edge of the sidewalk. They begin work at 7:30 A. M., and cease at 4:30 P. M. in winter, and at 5 P. M. in summer. On the more important streets they are kept at work three hours later, with excellent effect. The sweeping, by hand and with machines, is done entirely at night, after eight o'clock, when carriage traffic is nearly over. It continues until eight or nine in the morning. The streets are thus subjected to almost continuous hand-cleansing. In addition to this, when the weather is suitable, and when it is useful to do so, they are washed with the hose and jet. This must always be done late at night, when nearly all carriage traffic has ceased.

The courts and alleys occupied by the poorer classes are cleaned every day by the manual forces, and from April to October they are washed two or three times a week. Some places are washed nearly every night throughout the year. About 25,000,000 U. S. gallons of water are used in this way.

The sidewalks are swept as occasion requires, and in hot weather they are cleaned with squeegees in the daytime. The collection of street-sweepings, refuse, and rubbish is very large, and is increasing, as is the cost of the work. In 1895 there were collected 30,812 loads of "street-sweepings and slop," and 41,821 loads of house and trade refuse. The total removal of the year averages 233 loads per day for six days in the week. The engineer reports, with regard to trade refuse, that the habit of throwing it "into the dust-bins or other receptacles which should be used only for the ashes and ordinary house refuse appears to be much on the increase; and if this continues it must add largely to the cost of collection and the difficulty of getting rid of it when collected. It never was contemplated that the commission should remove trade refuse without being adequately paid for it. To do so is to benefit particular traders at the expense of the citizens generally."

I ask for this quotation the very thoughtful attention of those "traders" in New York who feel themselves greatly aggrieved if the city ash-carts are even slow or irregular in removing the refuse of their business. The complainers are always "taxpayers," but they seem to disregard the right of their fellow-citizens not to have their taxes saddled with the cost of other men's business processes.

The collections of all kinds are taken to a wharf on

the south side of the Thames, where they are roughly sorted. What is valuable as manure is boated away to the country. All else, after the salable refuse is culled out, is shot into a "destructor," or cremator. This apparatus works day and night throughout the year, save for from fifteen to twenty days, when it is stopped for repairs and cleaning. By the last report, it destroyed in the year 23,117 loads (66 loads per day), leaving about 22½ per cent. of "ashes and clinkers, more or less hard, but valueless, and for the removal of which the commission had to pay."

As is the case in so many other places, the question of final disposition is engaging the very serious attention of the authorities. In competition with concentrated fertilizers, street manure will not bear distant transportation. As populations grow larger the increasing output adds to the difficulty, and there seems to be no escape from the requirement for the conversion of the material into an inoffensive product, by an inoffensive process, within a practicable distance of the point of production.

English opinion seems to have become fixed on cremation as the only adequate means of relief. At the same time, it is not yet shown that cremation can be carried on without giving rise to nuisance, or at least to annoyance. Mr. Codrington, engineering inspector of the Local Government Board, in his report of 1888 as to twenty depots at which destructors had been erected, said, "Experience has shown that town refuse can be effectually burned in destructors and other furnaces without causing nuisance or offense at or about the works themselves"; but he adds that complaints are received of "fine dust and sometimes of charred paper proceeding from the chimney and falling at some little distance off," also of "an offensive smell, which, under certain conditions of the atmosphere, can be recognized at some distance on the leeward side of the chimney." If the chimney is built high enough to protect the immediate neighborhood the annoyance is only carried to more distant points. The only thing that is clear about the whole matter is that municipalities will have to face a greatly increased outlay to protect the people against the results of the increased production of wastes which *must* be got rid of, and the cost of whose disposal advances in progressive ratio as the material to be dealt with grows greater.

In 1893 the medical officer and the engineer of the London County Council made a report on "dust-destructors"—"dust" being the English for all manner of household wastes. It was calculated that the yearly quantity collected amounts to "about 260 tons per 1000 of the population." This would be about 1,300,000 tons for all London, or about 580 pounds for each person.*

The analysis of the material shows that it contains about eight per cent. (or 104,000 tons) of what would be salable in New York, including paper, bottles, broken glass, tin cans, bones, rags, and metals. No account is here made of wood, rubber shoes, leather shoes, hats, corks, strings, and some other trifles which are culled for sale by the scow-trimmers of New York.

At depots where cremation is not in use the method of handling is essentially the same as that described by Dr. Ballard in his report to the medical officer of the Local Government Board in 1878, which is briefly as follows:

The dust is dumped in the yard, where men and boys

* The annual output in New York is not far from 1250 pounds per person.

proceed to sort it, dragging the heap over with forks and rakes, collecting the bones, rags, etc. These are assorted into heaps and baskets. What is left is sifted to recover the bits of unburned coal. "The sifting is performed usually by women, who sit on or close to the heaps, having one or more baskets by their side and a riddle in their hands. A shovelful from the heap is shaken in the riddle, and the ashes and dust having passed through, what remains on the riddle is examined, and bones, potatoes, bits of iron, etc., not removed by the first dragging process are picked out." The coal and coke are thrown on a separate heap. He says: "The sorting process is a degrading occupation. The women employed are often seen covered almost to the waist with refuse, and they continually inhale into their lungs air polluted by the surrounding accumulations of dust." Large heaps of material are almost always to be found in the contractors' yards. The removal by barge, on which London is so dependent, is often interrupted by ice; the cargoes taint the air along the banks of the canals; and even when they reach their destination, the question of rendering them innocuous is still unanswered. The natural solution is to shoot the stuff "in some sparsely inhabited district where public opinion is not strong enough effectually to resent its being deposited." This was written nearly twenty years ago, and the case has grown worse year by year.

The report of 1893 says: "The merit of the destructor is, however, in a sense the main drawback to its popularity. The old system enjoys the great advantage that it quickly removes all cause of offense from general view, and few persons trouble themselves about the railway-siding or the canal wharf or the shoot in the country.

The destructor, if it is to establish the claim that it deals with the refuse from the outset, must be situated near inhabited houses, and its chimney cannot fail to excite attention. Again, if the destructor causes nuisance, it will mainly affect those living at a considerable distance from it, and thus it excites opposition, not of the inhabitants of houses in the poorer districts, which presumably exist in the neighborhood of the depot, but of the richer and much more critical population living half a mile or a mile away. It thus happens that, while few complaints are received concerning crude forms of furnace with short chimney-shafts, such as are found in many dust-yards and are used sometimes merely for burning paper, sometimes for dealing with vegetable refuse and ordinary house dust, considerable objection is made to much more perfect appliances furnished with lofty chimney-shafts." The final conclusion is that every appliance should be of the best and should be carefully worked and managed, "and under these conditions we think that the destruction of refuse by fire may be effected with success and without the production of nuisance."

The City is more important than any other single district of London; but it will not be without interest to refer briefly to the parish of Paddington, which has its disposal-works on the basin of a canal connecting with the system by which the northern part of London is served, and whence barges are sent into the country.

Paddington wharf was suggested to me as a good point to visit, because it has not only the depot of the parish itself, but also the works of two contractors who clean the parishes of St. George (Hanover Square), St. James, and Marylebone. Simple machinery, supplemented by hand-labor, is used in the sorting. At the Paddington depot, which is well paved and drained and well kept, 27 hands are employed, about half of the number being women. The work is carried on under cover. During the year (1895–96) 27,445 loads of dust were collected. The weekly range of loads was from 383 to 663. There were abstracted from this 313½ (gross) tons of salable material, as follows: coal, 9 tons; bones, 55 tons; rags, 144 tons; iron, 60 tons; various other metals, 4½ tons; white glass, 14 tons; colored glass, 36 tons.

The scrapings and sweepings from the streets are shot directly into the boats. "Slop" from wet streets goes first into a sort of cage, from which the dirty ooze runs into the canal, the more solid residue being boated away at a cost, including carting, boating, and unloading, of 47 cents per ton.

At the contractors' wharves the same conditions prevail, but there was rather less neatness of management. No statistics were to be had concerning their operations. They are under control of the vestry as to matters of nuisance.

The collection of dust in Paddington was until recently made only when a card with the letter "D" was exposed in the window; but the County Council now enforces a by-law requiring the sanitary authority of the parish to "cause to be removed not less frequently than once in every week the house refuse produced on the premises." The medical officer says that the system appears to work very satisfactorily, but at an increased cost.

The street-cleaning is carried out by gangs of sweepers, with horse-machines for scraping and sweeping. Main thoroughfares and important streets are swept daily, especially those paved with wood. Other streets of less traffic are swept two or three times a week. Slippery pavements are sanded, especially in frosty weather.

The general appearance of the streets in London as to cleanliness is much the same as that in New York so far as its more important thoroughfares are concerned. There is about the same amount of littering with paper and other refuse. The less important streets, which are swept only twice or thrice a week, are not so clean as ours, which are all swept at least once every day. But the pavement of London is *much* better.

BIRMINGHAM

Birmingham is a great, fine, dull, humdrum town, with about one quarter of the population of New York. So it must strike the visitor who comes to it fresh from the greater continental cities and from London. To the student of municipal administration it reveals a perfection of system, of executive completeness, and of economy which, if his standards have been formed in America, is simply amazing. It is well kept in all respects; yet the total appropriation for its Department of Public Works, including maintenance and all repairs of roadways, street-cleaning, the disposal of wastes, the care of the sewers, flushing and street-sprinkling, all stable expenses, including renewal of plant and stock, public lighting, and providing and maintaining of urinals, etc., for the year 1896–97, is, after crediting certain items of income, only $503,000. This result is possible only because of the perfect business management of all city affairs. Such economy will never be possible here so long as "politics" has anything whatever to do with our municipal administration. Naturally the lower rate of wages in England accounts for much of the saving; but the rate there is only about fifty per cent. less than it is here, and, at most, the payment of our wages would not raise the total outlay as above to more than $800,000.

The work in the str.ets, including repairs of pavement and macadam, sweeping and removal of sweepings, and all sprinklings, employs about 400 men (who work 54 hours per week) and about 160 horses. The gang-leaders are paid from $6 to $7 per week, drivers get from $5.50 to $6, and sweepers, $5.25. Selected men of this force do the road-repairing, being paid, in addition to their regular wages, a price by the piece for this work.

There are about 250 miles of street, of which about 40 miles are swept daily, 100 miles thrice a week, 100 miles twice a week, and 10 miles once a week.

There is one chief (road-surveyor) over the whole work, who is paid $2500 per year, and six district foremen, who get nearly $600 per year.

Most of the more important streets are paved with wood. This becomes very slippery, and it is regularly sanded with a crushed "grit," having some fragments of broken quartz or flint as large as peas and hazelnuts. This is spread from a cart with a shovel, and the men who do this work are so expert that they can make an effective covering of the whole street (30 to 45 feet wide) with the use of only 1 load to the mile. In Fifth Avenue, last winter, the contractor was restricted to the use of 4 loads per block, which would be 80 loads to the mile. There is no record of the amount used, but there is a vivid recollection in the Department of Street-Cleaning that it was enormous. Probably the day is not distant when we shall have to sand at least our asphalt streets, and it is a comfort to know that the quantity of sand used need not constitute an embarrassment to the work of cleaning. It is to be hoped, too, that the example of Birmingham may be heeded by the managers of our street-railways, which are now sanded with a wonderfully lavish hand.

Birmingham has a very large proportion of macadamized roadway, and it is of most excellent quality, well made, and *constantly* kept in repair. The work is done by the city's own force, and nothing is shirked. In minor streets the macadam is 21 feet wide. It is 4 inches higher at the center than at the edges. The material is 20 inches deep. The bed is graded to a true form and is rolled. The bottom layer, 8 inches thick, consists of *damp* ashes, rolled. On this is placed an 8-inch layer of gravel or broken slag, also rolled. Then follows a covering of "ragstone," or granite crushed to pass through a 2½-inch ring; this is rolled dry. Next comes a "binding" of crushed grit, which is rolled in wet, but not too wet, and is worked into the stone as thoroughly as possible. This makes a capital road, which is easily cleaned by scraping, and by sweeping with the birch-broom.

The most interesting part of the cleaning work of this city is that which has to do with the disposal of its wastes. Only about one half of its population is supplied with water-closets. The other half still use out-of-door "conveniences." These are supplied with "pans," which are regularly removed. There are about 36,000 of these. They are cylindrical in shape, 18 inches in diameter, and 15 inches deep. Household slops are not emptied into them. The pans are removed once a week. The removal is at night, from 10 P. M. to 8 A. M. They are covered with closely fitting covers, and are carried in closed vans, which take 18 at a time, and which have a receptacle at the tail end into which ash-tub refuse is emptied. The average weight of a van, when fully loaded, is about 8500 pounds.

There are three well-equipped yards, adjacent to canals, to which the pans are taken. One of these I visited. The van starts out from the yard with 18 clean pans, which are left in the privies from which the used ones are removed. On returning to the yard the pans are emptied into tanks, and are then turned over to the washers, who see that each van is supplied with clean pans to take out. The vans make from three to five journeys a night. This collection employs 61 horses and 122 men.

For the collection of dry refuse from shops and from houses which are furnished with water-closets (where no pans are used) 33 horses and 66 men are employed. This work is done in the daytime. The total weight of the dry refuse collected is about 35,000 tons per year. In the emptying of ash-pits on private premises, of which a considerable number still remain, 40 horses and 74 men are employed. The material thus collected amounts to about 50,000 tons in the year. Much of this is valueless as manure, less than 20,000 tons being used.

The making of fertilizers is an important part of the work. The dry refuse is screened in rotating screens, which separate the fine ash from the coarser parts, from which tin cans, broken crockery, etc., are picked out by hand. Rags are not saved. Part of the fine ash is mixed as an absorbent with the contents of the pans, and is sold as manure, being run from the mixing-machines directly into boats. The demand for this is decreasing, as concentrated fertilizers are gaining in favor with farmers.

The combustible material, including garbage, is burned in destructors, or cremating-furnaces, of which the city has about 50 in operation. The heat of these furnaces generates steam, which is used to evaporate the moisture of the pan contents, making a concentrated manure, and to furnish power to drive the mixing machinery, etc. The refuse passed through the furnaces is reduced to about thirty per cent. of its original weight. The clinker produced is employed for various purposes. Much is used by builders for concrete and mortar. It is also extensively used in road-making. As it is entirely free from offensive matter, it can be used without objection for filling low lands, for building roads, etc. The quantity burned in each furnace is given as 36½ tons per week (132 hours).

So much of the pan contents as is not mixed with ashes and so sold is manufactured into a highly concentrated manure by evaporation. The raw material is emptied into tanks, where it is treated with sulphuric acid to fix the ammonia against evaporation. From these it is run into other tanks over the drying-machines. These contain pipes which carry the vapors from the driers. The exhaust steam from the engines is similarly utilized, raising the contents of the tanks to near the boiling-point.

The steam-jacketed drying-machines consist of cylinders 8 feet in diameter and 13 feet long. Each has a hollow shaft, through which steam passes. They are also provided with revolving arms for stirring the contents and preventing them from forming into lumps. Suitable scrapers prevent the collection of drying matters on the surfaces. The foul vapor of the machines is arrested in a Liebig condenser. The water of condensation passes to the sewer in a nearly inodorous condition, and the gases are passed through the fire. After evaporation the dried material is ground in a mill.

The working charge of the machine is 16 tons, and the dry manure resulting weighs about 1¼ tons. From 800 to 1000 tons are produced each year. It sells for about $30 per ton.

By the statistics of 1892, the total refuse collected was 185,200 tons (of 2240 pounds). This was disposed of as follows:

	Tons.
Sent to dumps away from the city by boats	16,753
Sent to dumps by carts	7,515
Burned in furnaces	74,243
Manure sold, or wasted at dumps . . .	86,689
Total	185,200

The city owns and operates 34 canal-boats. None of the work is done by contract. It is found that under business management the agents of the administration can secure the greatest economy.

The items of receipts referred to in the early part of this paper do not include the sale of fertilizers. No reference to this is made in the annual estimates of the department. It is probably, like our own receipts from scow-trimming, paid into the general fund.

The chief lesson to be learned from Birmingham—and its methods are duplicated in English towns generally—is the lesson of non-political, non-shirking, and non-poor-man-coddling business management of public affairs. It shows us that a department of public works should not be a department of charities, and that—aside from proper and generous public charity—the money of the taxpayer should be used with the same care and economy that are so imperatively necessary to the successful management of private works.

A word of explanation is proper as to the "poor-man" element of the problem, and it applies to the question of public wages as well. The sympathies of all must be moved by the needs of the pauper class. The class that is obliged to work at hard labor is the happiest class in the community when it has employment, and sympathy for it should be limited to its fears for a rainy day and to its unsatisfied laudable ambition to get ahead in the world. All must desire security and relief for the one and advancement for the other. The best way to secure these is through the general prosperity of the community. This cannot be advanced by favoring a special few who are lucky enough to get a place on the city pay-roll, at the cost of the multitude who have to pay the shot. Fair wages for honest work is all that a wise and beneficent government can properly give to any man from the public purse, unless he is a pauper who must be kept from suffering. Too good a chance for the poor man only crowds the ranks with those who flock in from abroad, and it makes life all the harder for those with whom these come into competition.

BRUSSELS

New York has about ten times the population of Brussels and about six times the amount of street to be cleaned. The cost of street-cleaning in New York is $3,000,000; in Brussels it is $100,000 (500,000 francs). The cost per person of the population here is about $1.50; there it is about 50 cents. The cost per mile here is about $7000; there it is $1350. Wages here are $2 per day; there they are 50 cents per day.

Disregarding wages, and making the comparison by day's work, we find that in New York the working-force equals 5½ men per mile of street, while the Brussels force is $4\frac{6}{10}$ men per mile.

The work in Brussels is excellently well done, and the whole administration is good. It is all under the control of one director, Mr. Smeyers, who has organized the entire service, and who has won great credit for it. The work comprises:

1. The sweeping of all the streets and public places, and the cleansing of the outlying park, the Bois de la Cambre.
2. The removal of all sweepings and house wastes.
3. Street-sprinkling, and the flushing of streets, alleys, and courts.
4. The cleansing of sewer inlets.
5. The care of urinals.
6. Disinfection on the public highways.
7. The collection and removal of the wastes of the abattoir and of the fish-market.
8. The removal of snow and ice.
9. The sale of the collections for fertilizing, or their removal to a depot some four miles from the city, on the canal to the Scheldt.
10. The administration of the personnel of the service, the manufacture and maintenance of carts, tools, etc., the purchase of horses and forage, etc.

N. B. It is forbidden to discharge any street-sweepings into the sewers.

The department dates back to 1560, when the wastes of the town were deposited at the point now occupied by the main depot. Since 1853 the work has been greatly improved and systematized.

The present station and the canal basin were completed in 1865. Formerly the street-cleaning was done by a contractor, who paid the city for the privilege, selling the manure, etc., on his own account. The city received 6960 francs in 1836, the amount increasing until in 1846 it reached 26,940 francs. Later the work was taken in hand by the city, and the profit reached 75,505 francs in 1856. The construction and use of sewers soon reduced the amount of night-soil to be collected and sold, and as the sanitary condition improved the financial returns fell off. The people, too, became more and more exacting in the matter of complete sweeping and better sprinkling, so that in 1858 there was a net outlay of 11,950 francs, which by 1865 had grown to 102,000 francs. This led the Council to let out the work for an annual payment by the city of 81,000 francs.

Experience showed that this was not a good plan. There was a perfect deluge of reclamations and of complaints of bad service, and public dissatisfaction became so great that in 1871 the city again undertook the work on its own account, with the satisfactory results that have continued until this day.

The limited size of the city allows the concentration of all the main appliances of the service at one point, the Quai de la Voierie, near the custom-house, in the northwest part of the city. A large basin has been formed in connection with the canal, and the buildings of the department are separated from this by a broad esplanade. The carts, wagons, sweeping-machines, and water-carts are stored in the building. There is stabling for the 80 horses used, the necessary storage-room and shops, and a destructor, recently built on the English model. There are residences and offices for the director and his staff, and the whole establishment has the well-kept air of a military post. Eight iron canal-boats constitute the removal fleet. These are loaded from the carts along the esplanade. The refuse is picked over by the men themselves, and they are allowed to sell what they cull out for their own account. The sweeping of the streets is done mainly by hand, with the occasional accessory use of sweeping-machines, which work only at night. The city is divided into eleven sections, and the outlying park forms a twelfth. Each section has its supervisor, who is responsible for all details of its work to the director, who is in turn accountable to the magistrate of public works.

The supervisors work in accordance with certain general regulations, but they are allowed much discretion as to methods, as the conditions to be met are very various.

The work of sweeping, sprinkling, flushing, and disinfection begins at four in summer and at five in winter. It continues, according to needs, until three or four in the afternoon. A half-hour is allowed for breakfast, and an hour for the midday meal. On Sunday work ceases at eleven. The sweepers work in groups on the heaviest part of the work during the first two hours of the day.

At six in summer and at seven in winter the collection with the carts begins. The groups of sweepers are then broken up; about seventy of them are detailed to help the drivers to load their carts, and the others repair to their appointed routes, which they care for during the rest of the day. Some of them sprinkle the main streets, the boulevards, and the roads of the Bois de la Cambre with the hose and jet. The streets are sprinkled throughout the day with water-carts.

For the collection of house wastes the city is divided into 68 routes, each having its own cart, which makes two or three trips, according to distance. The carts take up the sweepings as they go. They are very large, and the loads average $2\frac{4}{10}$ cubic yards, which is about one half more than the New York load. The house collections are finished about ten or eleven o'clock, except on Fridays and Saturdays, when they may last a couple of hours longer.

The sprinkling of the streets is mainly done by drivers selected from among those who have cleaned up their routes. In dry weather the sweepers sprinkle with the hose the spaces which they are to sweep. This early sprinkling, the flushing of gutters, and the washing of courts make it possible to delay the use of the water-carts until somewhat late in the day. It is estimated that from April to September 1,000,000 gallons of water are used daily for the street service.

In each section one man has the care of the urinals; he is also charged with the disinfection of all places in his section which require such treatment.

The removal of the detritus of the abattoir and of the fish-market is, as far as possible, done at night, with covered wagons specially constructed for the purpose.

Concerning the removal of snow and ice, as I had no occasion to see its actual performance, I translate all that is said about it in the director's memorandum of the service:

"To effect the prompt disappearance of snow, its melting is secured with the aid of salt, containing at least ninety per cent. of chloride of sodium. This salt costs about four dollars per ton.

"The use of salt has sometimes been criticized. Its use in Brussels is justified by its economy, and also because the city has in its territory not a single place where the snow taken from the streets could be piled; it would all have to be dumped into the covered river (la Senne) which lies under the central boulevards. Fourteen manholes for this purpose have been built in the arch. The extraordinary work that has to be done in time of snow is the subject of a special organization, conforming to the depth of the fall. On such occasions the administration gathers all men out of work who are capable of holding a shovel or a broom. These are very numerous at this season of the year."

The collected wastes are offered for sale as manure at a tariff of prices fixed by the Administration of the Commune. It is mainly sent out in boats. What fails to find a purchaser is sent about four miles out on the canal and deposited on city property at Schaerbeek.

Assorted sweepings are offered "free on board" cars at Schaerbeek for 40 cents per ton. Its agricultural value, by analysis, is two or three times this price. Another notice informs those who live in the city or its suburbs that the department will furnish the same material by the cart-load at their residences; and that it is an "excellent manure for lawns, vegetable-gardens, pleasure-gardens, and greenhouses." The price is according to distance, the minimum being 80 cents per ton. The sales in 1894 amounted to $11,330, which was twelve per cent. of the net expense of the street-cleaning service.

The authorities of Brussels have paid much attention to the question of cremation, to be applied not only to garbage and other offensive matters, but to the whole mass of material collected by the department. A commission was sent to England in 1887 to examine the methods there in use. They reported in favor of the adoption of the system then working at Leeds, this to be applied to all the wastes in times of epidemic. In the absence of this condition, only so much would be cremated as could not be sold.

The conclusions of the commission were the subject of a long discussion in 1891, and were adopted by a vote of seventeen to four.

The report of 1894 describes the installation of two furnaces, built together, having a combined length of 37½ feet, a width of 14½ feet, and a height of 13½ feet. These furnaces stand near the stables on the north side of the yard, opposite to the weigh-bridge. They are found to answer a good purpose, and they are to be added to until capacity is secured sufficient for the incineration of the entire output in time of need.

A careful examination of the street-cleaning organization of Brussels produces the impressions of great completeness and of most careful and successful administration. It is, taken all in all, the best thing of its kind that I found during my investigations. The reason for its success is not far to seek. It is the result of that "aristocracy in official affairs" that our politicians are wont to decry when they discuss civil-service reform. It is due to the fact that every man in the service is assured of the stability of his position, and is safe in devoting his entire thought and energy to his work. "Rotation in office" and "the expiration of his term of appointment" do not disturb him. He need only do his work well and faithfully, and his future is assured. He is very ill paid from our standpoint, but he can live comfortably on his pay, and he is well cared for and well thought of.

The benefit fund of the department in 1894 received from its members $1272, the city added $1228, and other receipts swelled the total to $2837.

It paid to those who were sick $1970; doctors' fees, $343; medicine and surgery, $330; funeral expenses, $58; special aid to workmen, $91; expenses, $7.60; in all, $2799.60.

"N. B. The delegates of the workmen have had four meetings in the year 1894, in which they have been able to assure themselves that no expense foreign to the aims of the institution has been carried into the account."

MUNICH, COLOGNE, TURIN, AND GENOA

The only remaining places visited concerning which it seems to be worth while to give an account are Munich, Cologne, Turin, and Genoa.

The work in Munich is noticeable chiefly for its negative qualities. The streets are kept in very fair condition, mainly by contractors, the city doing the work on asphalt streets—a limited area—and charging the cost to the property-owners. As a rule, nearly the whole service that is performed by the Department of Street-Cleaning in New York is in Munich done by contractors employed and paid by private individuals. The street-railway companies clean their own tracks and the space between the rails. This is done, and very well done, by sturdy young women. They wore, last summer, no distinctive dress, but were distinguished by a uniform straw hat.

Cologne was a great surprise to me. I remembered its condition twenty-five years ago, and had had very little occasion to notice it since. I found it scrupulously clean—cleaner than any other place that I saw in Europe, not only in its central show parts, but in its outlying and more obscure quarters as well. My earlier observation had recalled Coleridge's lines:

The river Rhine, it is well known,
Doth wash your city of Cologne;
But tell me, nymphs! what power divine
Shall henceforth wash the river Rhine?

The "thousand and one stenches" for which the old city was noted have disappeared, and *eau de Cologne* no longer suggests a misnomer. The details of the method of work are similar to those of other continental cities and very similar to our own. The people seem to be well trained. Respect for the cleanliness of the streets has become a second nature. There is very little littering with paper and trash; receptacles are not set out long in advance of the arrival of the carts, and all of the details of the work and of the regulations by which it is directed are well thought out, well administered by the officials, and well received by the population.

Turin is very little behind Cologne in any respect. Its department is well organized, and here at last we found a distinctive street-cleaner's uniform, regularly worn and regularly inspected, and kept in good order. In winter the men wear high-crowned felt hats; in summer their hats, of the same shape, were of mixed straw, producing a light-brownish effect. The uniform is of a striped blue-and-white cotton goods, rather heavy, and rather given to fade under washing and exposure to the sun, but very good withal. The men trundle heavy hand-carts, after the manner of Vienna and Budapest, and the systems of collection and removal of sweepings are much the same. Turin covers a large area, and is the center of an active traffic, which brings many horses and mules into the city, in addition to the cavalry and artillery regiments stationed there. The ordinary work is done by 1 superintendent, 8 foremen, 84 special sweepers, 100 ordinary sweepers, and such a number of auxiliary sweepers as the work of the moment may require. These are usually needed only in emergencies. The pay of the superintendent is 60 cents per day; of the foremen, 50 cents; of the special sweepers, 45 cents; and of all others, 40 cents. The requirements for admission to the department are a knowledge of reading and writing, and age between 20 and 30 years, robust health, and a certificate of good character. The men are retired at the age of 40. Promotions are made for merit or by seniority. The most striking feature of the work in this city is its very low cost. The population was given to me as 340,000. Yet the whole expense of the department is only 532,500 lire (about $96,000). This is divided as follows:

The chief inspector	2,500	lire
Sweeping and carting	220,000	"
Sprinkling	85,000	"
Tools and material	25,000	"
The removal of snow and ice	200,000	"

There are in the city and its suburbs about 8600 horses and mules.

Genoa differs little from Turin in its methods of street-cleaning, and is not very far behind it in the matter of tidiness and cleanliness. Its condition, as I saw it, was very satisfactory, and Americans living there told me that it is always kept in good order. It is evidently fully up to the general European standard. The marvel of it all is that the cost of its work should be so little. The wages of the workmen, the highest being only 40 cents per day, would seem not to be sufficient to account for the fact that the contractor who does the whole work has recently entered on a new engagement for four years, at an annual cost of $40,000.

Here, as in Turin, there are two classes of police—one for the care of the public safety, and one for the maintenance of order. The latter, who guard the condition of the streets, wear natty cloth caps and long coats, both black, and ornamented with black braid. They are armed with light canes topped with a heavy metal head like a slung-shot. This, or their dignified demeanor, commands great respect.

In reviewing the whole subject of European street-cleaning as it came under my observation, the most important and suggestive consideration is that which concerns the relation of the people to the work, and, largely as leading to that, the manner in which the police intervene to prevent the littering of the streets. The regulations in European towns are no better than ours; the laws and ordinances are substantially the same; but there is the immense difference that in Europe laws and ordinances mean something and are executed, while here they are treated as mere matters of form. The policeman in Turin would as soon think of letting a highwayman escape his notice and official attention as of disregarding a man who deliberately threw littering material into the street. I have seen policemen in Europe accost gentlemen, apparently foreigners, and politely but effectively request them to pick up papers they had thrown away. I have seen policemen in New York—and the spectacle is observable at every turn—saunter in a dignified manner past a crowd of littering people, utterly unconscious of the fact that they were violating any rule or regulation, and apparently considering it beneath the dignity of their position to heed the suggestion of a citizen that they were not obeying their orders. Here lies unquestionably the great secret of the difference between our ways and European ways.

As to methods available for the improvement of the New York system, very little was observed. As a rule, our carts are better than theirs, being lighter and tighter; our brooms are probably better; and our methods of final disposition are quite as good, owing, no doubt, to our much better conditions for dumping refuse. Indeed, the only country in which important differences were found was Austria. The method of separating wastes at the point of final disposition in operation at Budapest was suggestive of very important improvements available here. So in Vienna I found the best street-sweeping machine, the best sprinkling-cart, and the best snow-plow. All of these will be tried here, and adopted if found sufficiently better than what we are now using.

Another matter of especial interest to New-Yorkers is that our system of street-sprinkling is entirely unique. So far as I could learn, the world has never before conceived of such a method—where only that part of the street lying in front of property whose owner pays the private contractor a sprinkling-rate gets any sprinkling whatever, and where the volume of water used is regulated by the sweet will of the driver, without restraint from any official authority. In Europe street-sprinkling is always under the control of the authority by which street-cleaning is regulated. It is a necessary and inseparable part of the same work. There is a proposition now before our legislature to extend and to increase the street-sprinkling monopoly of this city. I trust that the people will insist on the defeat of this measure, and so avoid the further tying up of their interests in this respect with the financial interests of a street-drenching company with a pull, as at present. There is no more reason for farming out the work of sprinkling the streets than that of sweeping them. Both are functions of the municipal authorities, and should be kept under close control.

CHAPTER XIV

THE JUVENILE STREET-CLEANING LEAGUES

BY DAVID WILLARD, D. S. C., SUPERVISOR

TO arouse a civic pride among New-Yorkers is not distinctly within the province of the Department of Street-Cleaning. It is desirable, however, that an interest in the observation of the simple necessary rules of the Sanitary Code be awakened in the minds of at least the ignorant foreign population crowded into the East Side districts. To use for this end the influence of the children, who are recognized by their parents as superior to them in education and intelligence, is not a new idea, but one practically untried to any extent. The fund of patriotism with which every child of school age is endowed constantly shows itself, and always with great strength. It is unfailing when drawn upon for the city's interests. Noting the zeal with which children have given themselves to such patriotic organizations as the Civic History clubs, and the equally excellent moral Association, the Anti-Cigarette League, it seemed possible to enlist their interest in the cleanliness of the city.

A beginning was made in the lower East Side under the auspices of the University Settlement. A number of boys from the tenth and eleventh wards were organized into a club by a detailed Inspector of the department. Shortly after, two more were started at the Educational Alliance in East Broadway; and these were followed by one or more on the West Side and several in the upper part of the city. The plan of organization adopted was parliamentary in its nature; officers were elected, a constitution prepared with a stated object "to keep the streets in a clean and healthful condition," and regular weekly business meetings were held. During these meetings there was a discussion of such subjects as related to the health and cleanliness of the city. The club members were encouraged to report, on official blanks furnished them for the purpose, any work that they might have accomplished in the way of removing litter from the streets, inducing others not to throw out refuse, or noting certain blocks or houses where the people were careless in their habits or had a disregard for the sanitary laws.

The movement was very popular with the children from the start. "Please may we have a club?" became a constant, almost daily, demand from committees of urchins all over the city. One such band came in one day with the same question. "And why do you wish a club?" said I. "Oh, the boys by our block they knock banana-shells and all dirty things in the street, and we want to reform them." "But perhaps the boys are very bad and don't want to be reformed," I suggested. "Oh, yes, they do," the little leader replied. "We asked them, and they all said they did."

As institutions and missions came forward offering

their rooms and requesting us to visit and address the children they gathered together, we were able to extend the work greatly. Many volunteer directors also organized clubs under our supervision, and thus spread our system and its influence.

In the winter of 1896–97 the work gained such wide and favorable notice that certain civic organizations in Boston and Chicago sent representatives to investigate our methods for the purpose of starting similar work in those cities. Philadelphia, Brooklyn, Pittsburg, Utica, Denver, and numerous small cities and towns are taking up the idea, and report most satisfactory results.

This past summer, by an arrangement with the Association for Improving the Condition of the Poor, five classes in the Norfolk Street Vacation School were organized as miniature departments of street-cleaning, for such work as that done by the outside clubs. So successful did this new style of organization prove that the Board of Education authorized its introduction into all of the city schools of the four higher grades.

The matter of clean streets is brought to the attention of the child in the class-room by short talks with fitting illustrations and anecdotes. He is made to feel a sense of personal possession in relation to the streets, which will cause him to keep from doing them an injury and also make him resent their littering by other people. Personal pride and patriotic feeling are stirred, and the matter is brought closely home by showing that, of the hundreds who suffer from clogged and ill-smelling sewers, slippery banana-peels, mixed and disease-breeding garbage-barrels, the child's own parents or even he himself may any moment be among the number. Then, that the idea may be kept constantly fresh in the mind, an organization is formed which is modeled after the department in miniature. Every child is given a paper on which to record at the end of a week the number of persons or other children to whom he may have spoken about the matter of keeping the city tidy and neat; the number of bonfires which he has succeeded in stopping; the number of skins which he has kicked into the gutter from the sidewalk; the number of papers he has induced others to put in the barrel instead of on the pavement; and various things of a similar nature. On the basis of such reports, badges are given out, ranking the children as "Helpers," "Foremen," or "Superintendents." Special work and interest is rewarded by advancement and the assignment of some particular department title, together with a certificate of authorization from the commissioner made out after this form:

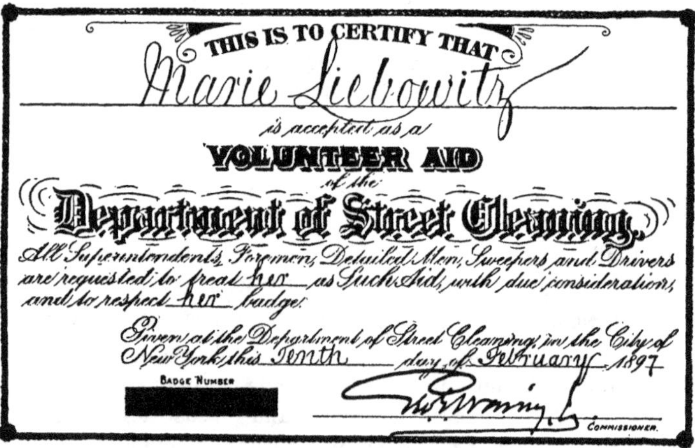

THIS IS TO CERTIFY THAT

Marie Liebowitz

is accepted as a

VOLUNTEER AID

of the

Department of Street Cleaning.

All Superintendents, Foremen, Detailed Men, Sweepers and Drivers are requested to treat her as such Aid, with due consideration, and to respect her badge.

Given at the Department of Street Cleaning, in the City of New York, this Tenth day of February 1897

BADGE NUMBER

COMMISSIONER.

The rank of Foremen is recruited from that of Helpers as fast as the Foremen are promoted to other offices or distinctions; and the Superintendents are elected every two months from the Foremen, who constitute an eligible class. To such arrangements the children lend themselves with great readiness, and a friendly rivalry stimulates everything which can tend toward such a betterment of civic conditions as may lie within a child's power. From time to time, under the auspices of some particular miniature department, large mass-meetings of children are held in some hall, where an opportunity is given to hear talks from various officials of the large department and to enjoy such simple entertainment as the children and their friends can offer.

The singing of "street-cleaning songs," of which these are among the number, adds zest to the enthusiasm of such meetings and has its share of influence:

AND WE WILL KEEP RIGHT ON

There 's a change within our city, great improvements in our
  day;
The streets' untidy litter with the dirt has passed away.
We children pick up papers, even while we are at play;
    And we will keep right on.

No longer will you see a child fall helpless in the street
Because some slippery peeling betrayed his trusting feet;
We do what we are able to make our sidewalks neat;
    And we will keep right on.

And all the people far and near, in sunshine or in rain,
Rejoice to see our cleaner streets, and find the reason plain:
We children take a hand to keep our thoroughfares so clean;
    And we will keep right on.

NEIGHBOR MINE

There are barrels in the hallways,
    Neighbor mine;
Pray be mindful of them always,
    Neighbor mine.
If you 're not devoid of feeling,
Quickly to those barrels stealing,
Throw in each banana-peeling,
    Neighbor mine!

Do not drop the fruit you 're eating,
    Neighbor mine,
On the sidewalks, sewer, or grating,
    Neighbor mine.
But, lest you and I should quarrel,
Listen to my little carol:
Go and toss it in the barrel,
    Neighbor mine!

Look! whene'er you drop a paper,
    Neighbor mine,
In the wind it cuts a caper,
    Neighbor mine.
Down the street it madly courses,
And should fill you with remorses
When you see it scare the horses,
    Neighbor mine!

Paper-cans were made for papers,
    Neighbor mine;
Let 's not have this fact escape us,
    Neighbor mine.
And if you will lend a hand,
Soon our city dear shall stand
As the cleanest in the land,
    Neighbor mine!

In this way large bodies of children are reached and interested, and the incentive is given to start new clubs and spread the work.

The principle on which all this is based has often been criticized on the ground that in thus appealing to children they are given an undue sense of their own importance in the school and city and that a tendency to spy upon and report the actions of other people is encouraged. This has not been the result, however, as everything looking toward such a condition is eliminated from the work. Emphasis is laid solely upon the child's individual responsibility to his own city and his own best self for the way in which he regards the streets and the example which he sets to others. The whole principle is embraced in the civic pledge which each club and department member learns and repeats.

CIVIC PLEDGE

We who are soon to be citizens of New York, the largest city on the American continent, desire to have her possess a name which is above all reproach. And we therefore agree to keep from littering her streets and as far as possible to prevent others from doing the same, in order that our city may be as clean as she is great and as pure as she is free.

The weekly reports, far from being complaints, are statistical statements of what any child may have accomplished. They form a basis for awarding badges, and lend formality to the movement, so that a child comes to feel that he is rendering to the city some recognized service. Many of the reports show a surprising amount of earnest work, and are themselves refutations of all criticism, as well as object-lessons in what can be done for children in the way of teaching them clean habits and stirring up in them a spirit of civic pride.

The following specimens are culled from the weekly reports:

"Col. Waring.

"Dear Sir:—While walking through Broome St., Monday, at 2:30 p. m., I saw a man throughing a mattress on the street. I came over to him and asked him if he had no other place to put it but here. He told me that he does not no any other place. So I told him in a barrel, he then picked it up and thanked me for the inflammation I gave him. I also picked up 35 banana skins, 43 water mellion shells, 2 bottles, 3 cans and a mattress from Norfolk St."—Metropolitan League.

"To Col. Waring. Distinguished a bon-fire in 5th St., between Av. C. & D."—Industrial League.

"I saw a man eating a banana. He took the skin and threw it on the sidewalk. I said to him please sir will you be so kind & pick it up and he said all right."—Juvenile Progress Club.

"There was a barrel full of paper on East B'way and when the cartman emptied the barrel a lot of small pieces of paper fell all over the side-walk. The housekeeper took the barrel in and did not even try to pick them up. I went up & asked her to pick them up and she refused. Then I asked her to loan me a broom and I would sweep. She consented and I swept. She was baking in her stove so I put the paper in the fire. While doing this she asked me who I was, and I told her I belonged to a club which is interested in having clean streets. She asked me if I had a badge and I told her we could try to keep the streets clean without a badge & she said we were right."—INDUSTRIAL LEAGUE.

"MR. E. WARING So I passed Grand St. so I saw paper at the side-walk so I told a Street Cleaner so he said I shall go to see Mr. E. Waring so I said I dont no where to find him, that was the second time that I saw that again. I passed Ludlow St. I saw a can dirt where it belongs garbage and it was nasty so I called a man. I passed Essex St. so I saw a lady throughing from the window apple skins down stairs on a lady's head, so I called up and she said she won't do it no more."—VACATION SCHOOL.

In sections of the city where the English language is but infrequently heard the children are often the only means of communication which parents have with outsiders. Thus the children's assistance in spreading a knowledge of the ordinances and the reasons for them is of no small value. This was keenly appreciated by the department at the time when the new law relative to the mixing of garbage went into effect. By the aid of the children we were able to translate this from its legal phrases into the vernacular and spread it by word of mouth from tenement to tenement, bringing about in a short time what would have taken regular inspectors some months to accomplish. As another instance of positive results attained by the children's aid, it is estimated, on the basis of their reports, that over six hundred bonfires have either been extinguished by them or called to the attention of the police within the last nine months. This makes a saving of several thousand dollars to the Department of Public Works in their bill for the laying of new pavements.

Still, if nothing is gained to the city except in a negative way, at least the neutrality of thousands of children has been purchased, and the streets are the cleaner from the fact that so many are kept from making them dirty. But for the child himself results are all on the positive side. The good it does him is not a matter of conjecture. He is cleaner in his person and in his habits, to which the report of many a school-teacher bears witness. And he cannot fail to grow up with an increased love for his city, the result of that knowledge which will make him the sturdy, upright citizen which the times demand in great measure.

CHAPTER XV

CONCLUSION

THE following was written in 1894 by Mr. J. S. Da Costa to a friend in Rio Janeiro:

"New York seems to be the dirtiest wealthy city that I have seen. There are portions of the city that are so packed with empty vehicles of every size and shape that one is apt to think, from a view of the filthy state of all their surroundings, that after eight o'clock at night the commercial portion of the city is converted into a huge dirty public stable, unsightly and disgustingly hideous, viewed from whatever point it may be looked at."

New York is now thoroughly clean in every part, the empty vehicles are gone, and no such criticism as that of our Brazilian writer will ever be made again. "Clean streets" means much more than the casual observer is apt to think. It has justly been said that "cleanliness is catching," and clean streets are leading to clean hallways and staircases and cleaner living-rooms. A recent writer says:

"It is not merely justification of a theory to say that the improvement noticed in the past two and a half years in the streets of New York has led to an improvement in the interior of its tenement-houses. A sense of personal pride has been awakened in the women and children, the results of which have long been noticeable to every one engaged in philanthropic work among the tenement dwellers. When, early in the present administration, a woman in the Five Points district was heard to say to another, 'Well, I don't care; my street is cleaner than yours is, anyhow,' it was felt that the battle was won."

Few realize the many minor ways in which the work of the department has benefited the people at large. For example, there is far less injury from dust to clothing, to furniture, and to goods in shops; mud is not tracked from the streets on to the sidewalks, and thence into the houses; boots require far less cleaning; the wearing of overshoes has been largely abandoned; wet feet and bedraggled skirts are mainly things of the past; and children now make free use as a playground of streets which were formerly impossible to them. "Scratches," a skin disease of horses due to mud and slush, used to entail very serious cost on truckmen and liverymen. It is now almost unknown. Horses used to "pick up a nail" with alarming frequency, and this caused great loss of service, and, like scratches, made the bill of the veterinary surgeon a serious matter. There are practically no nails now to be found in the streets.

The great, the almost inestimable, beneficial effect of the work of the department is shown in the large reduction of the death-rate and in the less keenly realized but still more important reduction in the sick-rate. As compared with the average death-rate of 26.78 of 1882–94, that of 1895 was 23.10, that of 1896 was 21.52, and that of the first half of 1897 was 19.63. If this latter figure is maintained throughout the year, there will have been fifteen thousand fewer deaths than there would have been had the average rate of the thirteen previous years prevailed. The report of the Board of Health for 1896, basing its calculations on diarrheal diseases in July, August, and September, in the filthiest wards, in the most crowded wards, and in the remainder of the city, shows a very marked reduction in all, and the largest reduction in the first two classes.

It is not maintained, of course, that this great saving of life and health is due to street-cleaning work alone. Much is to be ascribed to improvements of the methods of the Board of Health, and not a little to the condemnation and destruction of rear tenements; but the Board of Health itself credits a great share of the gain to this department.

An effort has been made to account for the better work done on the streets solely by the larger amount of money expended. But in the matter of cleaning there has been no such increase of cost. In studying this, it is proper to exclude the cost of "snow removal," and of the purchase of "new stock and plant," bought for permanent use and to repair waste due to the work of previous years. The expenditure for all other items, for all really "street-cleaning" accounts, was as follows for five years past:

		Percentage of increase
1892	$1,890,376.46	
1893	2,036,812.81	7.7
1894	*2,366,419.49	16.2
1895	2,704,577.26	14.3
1896	2,776,749.31	2.7

The increase in 1893–94 was 23.9.
" " " 1895–96 " 17.

* Includes $140,000 secured in judgments against the city for increase in wages.

Furthermore, during this administration the employment of private ash-carts and private sweepers has greatly decreased as people have found that the department service could be relied on.

However, suppose the work has cost more. It has been well and honestly done, and it has produced the results cited above. I accept cheerfully full responsibility for the outlay, and I should gladly spend still more if it were needed for the good of the people. And, after all, how much did it cost all the people of this city for all that was done in 1896, including the removal of snow and the renewal of "stock and plant"? The total sum is $3,283,-853.90. And how much is that?

It is almost exactly three cents per week for each one of us!

The progress thus far made is satisfactory. An inefficient and ill-equipped working-force, long held under the heel of the spoilsman, has been emancipated, organized, and brought to its best. It now constitutes a brigade three thousand strong, made up of well-trained and disciplined men, the representative soldiers of cleanliness and health, soldiers of the public, self-respecting and life-saving. These men are fighting daily battles with dirt, and are defending the health of the whole people. The trophies of their victories are all about us—in clean pavements, clean feet, uncontaminated air, a look of health on the faces of the people, and streets full of healthy children at play.

This is the outcome of two and a half years of strenuous effort—at first against official opposition and much public criticism. Two and a half years more, with a continuance of the present official favor and universal public approval, should bring our work to its perfection. It should make New York much the cleanest and should greatly help to make it the healthiest city in the world. By that time its death-rate should be reduced to 15 per thousand—which would mean for our present population a saving of sixty lives per day out of the one hundred and forty daily lost under the average of 26.78 (1882–94).

I venture to predict a recovery, from the sale of refuse material, of at least one half the cost of the whole work.

These diagrams set forth the actual relation between the work of former years and that of Mayor Strong's administration:

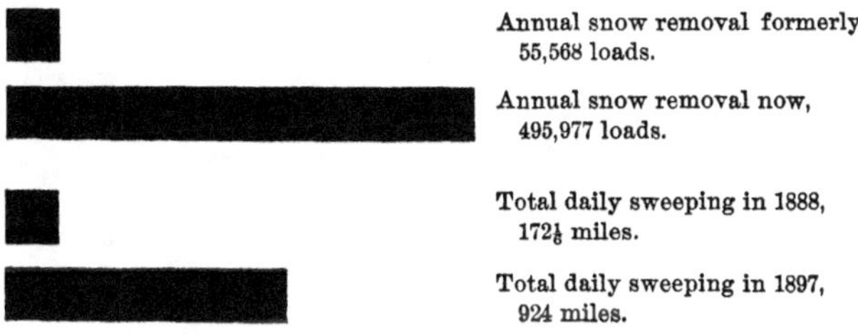

APPENDIX

HISTORICAL

THE Department of Street-Cleaning was created by an act of the Legislature, Chapter 367 of the Laws of 1881, passed May 26, 1881. It provided for the appointment of a commissioner of street-cleaning by the mayor, with the approval of the Board of Health, charged with the duty of causing the streets of New York to be thoroughly cleaned and kept clean at all times, and of removing or otherwise disposing of, as often as the public health and the use of the streets should require, all street-sweepings, ashes, and garbage, and of removing new-fallen snow from leading thoroughfares and such other streets and avenues as may be found practicable. Under this act, the commissioner of street-cleaning was empowered to let out special contracts, for periods not exceeding three years, for the work of street-sweeping and cleaning, or for the collection of ashes and garbage, or some part thereof, in particular districts, to be designated, such contracts to be approved by the Board of Estimate and Apportionment. He was also authorized to make special contracts for the final disposition of the material for a term of five years, if similarly approved.

James S. Coleman, the first commissioner under the new law, was appointed June 4, 1881. He held office until January 17, 1890. Mr. Coleman says:

"Early in 1882 it was decided, as a measure of economy, and to lighten the immediate cumbersome control of the extensive working-force and apparatus required for the whole city, and to insure the more frequent cleaning of the streets, to try the contract system of work in the territory lying south of Fourteenth Street, reserving that portion of the city north of Fourteenth Street for the operations of the department. The territory to be embraced in the contract system was divided into two districts, denominated respectively the first and second street-cleaning districts, the former lying west of Broadway and containing fifty miles of paved streets, and the latter east of Broadway and containing seventy-five miles of paved streets.

"In February, 1882, contracts were entered into for two years with C. F. Mairs to clean the first district at the rate of $132,000 per annum, and with F. Theodore Walton for the second district at $225,000 per annum. The streets were classified: those of the first class, being about five miles, were to be completely cleaned their entire length and width respectively once every twenty-four hours; those of the second class, being about thirty-two miles, were to be cleaned on alternate days; and the remainder, about seventy-eight miles, were to be cleaned twice a week. Besides, the contractors were obliged to remove all ashes and garbage from the streets of the districts every day; and when the streets could not be cleaned in the regular manner by reason of a heavy fall of snow, the contractors were obliged to employ their entire force of laborers and carts in removing snow and ice, cleaning cross-walks, clearing gutters, and generally preparing for a sudden thaw. . . .

"The contracts in existence in 1888 were entered into on May 1, 1886, for three years, with Hayward & Duffy for the first district at the rate of $117,490 per annum, and with Michael J. O'Reilly for the second district at the rate of $204,900 per annum. . . .

"In considering the contract system, it should be borne in mind that, notwithstanding the increase year by year in the amount of work to be done, comparing the terms of the first and the last contract, and in the amount of work that was accomplished, yet the cost to the city has been constantly reduced:

Contracts for 1882	. . . . .	$357,000.00
" " 1886	. . . . .	322,390.00"

Mr. Coleman in 1889 made an elaborate report of the work of the years 1887–88, with a review of the operations of the department from 1882.

He speaks of the impediments of the work as being "very numerous and of the most aggravating character, . . . such as badly paved streets, the want of proper receptacles for ashes and garbage, and innumerable street incumbrances of all kinds, . . . the more serious obstructions arising from the operations of various private corporations in laying down pipes, conduits, and other appliances, and making repairs to the various underground communications which they controlled. These corporations tore up the streets, dug trenches, threw the dirt carelessly on the carriageways, and piled paving-stones, lumber, and other constructional material on them, in defiance of the ordinances and against the protestations of the public. . . .

"The abuse of the streets was carried on to such intolerable dimensions that the grand jury made the suppression of it a matter of serious discussion, and even considered the advisability of indicting its promoters. The Academy of Medicine dissected the subject from a hygienic standpoint, and arrived at the conclusion that street excavations, to the extent that was then going on during the summer months, were liable to lead to severe outbreaks of malarial and intestinal diseases. The Board of Aldermen and the Chamber of Commerce also agitated the question of securing reform. The latter body held a conference in December with the mayor, when it was generally agreed that the first thing necessary was to give the commissioner of public works complete power to relay the pavements when opened by private companies. But the needful legislation for such a proceeding was, I regret to say, not enacted, and all the agitation on the subject resulted merely in vigorous protests and denunciations, and it was only with the actual arrival of winter that the destruction of the pavements ceased."

After reciting the city ordinances and the laws of the Health Department concerning the disposal of refuse by householders, Mr. Coleman says:

"The result of the non-observance and the non-enforcement of these laws was that the condition of the roadways, gutters, and sidewalks in the crowded tenement districts on the east and west sides of the city, in many instances, was exceedingly offensive in appearance. Notwithstanding the regular and well-directed daily labors of the street-cleaners, refuse of almost every sort could be seen, within an hour after the street had been regularly cleaned, lying loose on the street, showing that the rules of the Board of Health were not observed. Tenements containing twenty or thirty families (representing more than one hundred individuals) were supplied with only one receptacle (barrel, can, or tub) for the ashes and garbage, and, as a consequence, the greater part of the refuse was thrown on the street. There were many instances where no receptacle of any kind was used, and the household refuse was deliberately flung into the street. . . . The presence of ash-barrels on the sidewalks never fails to attract the attention of the ubiquitous rag-picker, who, hook in hand, rakes up and overhauls their contents, to the great disgust and annoyance of residents and passers-by. Such proceedings are a violation of Section 96 of the Sanitary Code, which states that no person not for that purpose authorized shall interfere with such receptacles or the contents thereof. . . .

"In previous years the experiment of collecting ashes and garbage at night was tried, so as, if possible, to abolish or abate the ash-barrel nuisance—the unsightly appearance, the offensive odor, and the annoyance to pedestrians (unavoidable in windy weather), incidental to the collection of ashes and garbage during the daytime. The trial failed because householders neglected to comply with the regulations requiring them to put out the receptacles at such hours and in such places as would render them accessible to the ashmen and facilitate the prosecution of their work."

Concerning vehicles in the streets Commissioner Coleman says, "It is safe to say that the number will reach close on fifty thousand, and for many of these obstructions there is no warrant of law whatever"; and as to the law regulating the deposit of building-material and rubbish in the streets: "It is notorious that this law is not complied with; and the material becomes spread over the street, and the neighborhood becomes an eyesore and an offense. High winds scatter the sand, and when rain falls, passing vehicles churn the earth into mud and distribute it along the street. Again, in numerous instances the material is so placed that the free flowage of water along the gutter is obstructed, and pools of stagnant water form on the streets."

The plant of the department consisted, in 1888, of "380 horses, 359 carts, 40 sweeping-machines, 20 sprinkling-carts, 3 snow-plows, 4 tug-boats, 42 scows.

"South of Fourteenth Street, in the territory under contract, the plant employed consisted of 18 sweeping-machines, 9 watering-carts, and from 135 to 190 horses and carts for the collection of street dirt and ashes and garbage."

The whole working-force of the department in 1888 numbered 896 men. The number employed by the contractors south of Fourteenth Street was 425. In addition to these, there were about 200 laborers unloading and trimming scows, making the whole force, in round numbers, 1500.

Horace Loomis held the office of commissioner from January 17, 1890, until April 4, 1890, when Hans S. Beattie was appointed. He was succeeded by Thomas S. Brennan, September 17, 1891.

The department was entirely reorganized by Chapter 269 of the Laws of 1892, approved April 9, 1892. The new organization was the outgrowth of an examination of the subject of street-cleaning made in 1891, at the request of Mayor Grant, by Messrs. Morris K. Jesup, Thatcher M. Adams, Charles F. Chandler, D. H. King, Jr., and Francis V. Greene.

On May 9, 1892, Mr. Brennan was reappointed under the new law. He was succeeded by William S. Andrews, July 21, 1893, and he by George E. Waring, Jr., January 15, 1895.

In his letter to Messrs. Jesup, Adams *et al.*, Mayor Grant asked the following questions:

"1. Is the Department of Street-Cleaning efficiently managed, and, if not, in what respect is it inefficient?

"2. Is the present law adequate, and, if not, what additional legislation is required?

"3. Is the amount of money now appropriated sufficient to clean the streets properly, and, if not, what, in your judgment, is necessary?"

In reply to the first question, the committee says:

"We reply that, in our opinion, it is not efficiently managed, our standard of comparison being the management of well-established private corporations engaged in large enterprises. We consider it inefficient in the following respects:

"1. In the employment of labor. It does not appear to have any proper system of selecting laborers and cartmen, or of permanently retaining those who are capable and hard-working. An effort was made last year by Commissioner Beattie to improve the method of selecting laborers; but after a short trial it was abandoned, for reasons stated by him in his letter to us of February 7 and in his conversation of February 20, both of which are given in the Appendix.

"It appears from the testimony of the same commissioner that it has been the custom of the department 'to have men appointed and removed principally at the whim of the person who makes the request,' and that the men are often employed only two-thirds time, i.e., only four days in the week, or six hours in the day. In our judgment, no public or private enterprise can be efficiently conducted with any such system, or lack of system, in selecting or keeping its employees.

"2. In the location of its plant.

"The department has only one stable, situated at Seventeenth Street and the East River. Here are kept all its machines, carts, horses, and tools. This point is about five miles from the paved streets of Harlem and three miles from the center of the down-town district. The average distance from the stable to the point where each cart and laborer does his work is about two miles, and probably one fifth of the time of the employees and animals is consumed in traveling back and forward over this distance. We consider such an arrangement as unsuitable as it would be to have all the apparatus of the Fire Department concentrated in one engine-house. . . .

"4. In the lack of proper organization and disposition of its force. . . . We have constantly observed, in one part of the city or another, where there were large piles of mud and dirt in the gutters heaped up but not removed for several days, owing either to lack of carts, lack of scows, or lack of proper direction. During this time the piles are strewn on the streets by vehicles or by the wind, and the work of cleaning has largely to be done over again. We consider this a waste of money. . . .

"There are minor points in which, in our judgment, the street-cleaning is inefficient, as will appear in the detailed memoranda in the Appendix; but the failure to obtain more satisfactory results with the $10,000,000 expended for street-cleaning in the last nine years is, in our opinion, due chiefly to the five causes above named and in the order stated."

The second question is practically answered as follows:

"We reply that, in our opinion, the present law is entirely adequate to secure the cleaning of the streets and keeping them clean, provided it is efficiently administered and the commissioner of street-cleaning has the active and cordial coöperation of the mayor, the police force and police justices, the Department of Health, the commissioner of public works, and the Board of Estimate and Apportionment. Without such coöperation at all times, no legislation, in our judgment, will secure clean streets. With it, the present law is sufficient."

Concerning the sufficiency of the appropriation the committee says:

"We reply that, in our opinion, the amount of money now appropriated is not sufficient, and that the sum necessary is about $1,800,000, as will appear more in detail in the estimate contained in the Appendix; and this amount should be increased from year to year in proportion to the increase in amount of material to be removed, which appears to be approximately five per cent. per year. In considering the question of necessary expense, we feel obliged to say that, in our opinion, the present system of employing laborers and cartmen is wasteful and extravagant. To keep the streets clean with such a system would require at least $2,500,000."

The following relates to the *employment of labor:*

"By the testimony of Commissioner Beattie before the Fassett Investigating Committee, and by his very frank conversation with this committee, abstracts of which are hereto annexed, a clear idea can be obtained of the system of employment of labor which he found in force in the Department of Street-Cleaning when he took office, and which to a large extent prevails there to-day.

"Briefly stated, that system is this: The department has, measurably speaking, little or nothing to do with the selection of its own employees.

"They are 'appointed and removed principally at the whim of persons' (unconnected with the department) 'making requests to that effect.'

"They are selected 'without reference to their ability to do the given work for which they are employed, and are liable to discharge without good business reasons therefor.'

"The employment of laborers by the department is in the hands of the deputy commissioner, and 'men come to him personally, or through their friends, or with their friends,—and their friends are men who take an active interest in these (public) matters, aldermen, assemblymen, etc.,—and apply to the deputy.'

"The pressure for employment is great, so great that 'there arises a disposition, even on the part of the foremen, to accommodate the requests that are made and the persons who make the requests; and no doubt it occasionally happens that a man who might be made a very good public servant is dropped with a view of increasing the number of places to be filled.'

"It appears also that the department is subjected to great pressure for employment of labor '*which is utterly worthless to it*,' by persons identified with charitable work, whose motives are unselfish, but who argue that the persons whose employment they advocate must be supported by the city as paupers if not as laborers.

"No examination as to fitness is made by the department 'beyond a casual examination of the man by the eye of the deputy or superintendent,' and no record is made of this casual examination.

"Once appointed, the laborer, however well conducted, has no assurance of permanent employment. Should the appropriation prove insufficient,—as is frequently the case,—or should it be injudiciously expended in the earlier part of the year and consequently become limited for the remainder, he is placed on short time, working six hours instead of eight, and four days instead of six.

"He is employed by the hour, paid only for time he is actually employed, at the rate of twenty-five cents per hour.

"If he works ten hours he thus receives $2.50; if eight hours, $2.

"In our judgment, such a system is at once inefficient, wasteful of the public money, and productive of bad results. No well-managed private corporation engaged in large industrial undertakings would employ a similar system. Other municipal departments employing large numbers of men do not use it. The members of the Police and Fire departments submit to examinations which must reveal certain fixed standards as conditions of employment. Once enrolled, they are certain, during good behavior, of permanent employment at a fixed wage.

"From both of these departments, especially from the latter, the city receives excellent service.

"It cannot expect an equal degree of excellence from any department whose system of employment is in such glaring contrast.

"When Commissioner Beattie was asked by us, 'Is the force of laborers obtained under the present system satisfactory to you?' he replied emphatically and decidedly, 'It is not.'

"That he is not alone in his judgment appears from the following extract from one of the many letters of the same tenor received by this committee. It is from a banker residing in Fifty-eighth Street between Madison and Park avenues.

"'For the past seven years I have daily crossed Fifth Avenue twice on my way to the elevated station. Scores of times have I watched the men on our block and Fifth Avenue; and as far as I could judge, their object seemed to be to accomplish as little work as possible. I don't hesitate to say that, as a general rule, four able-bodied men could in the same time, without extra exertion, accomplish the work of any ten men that I watched, and thus it is that hundreds of thousands of dollars are thrown away—lazy, aged, worn-out men employed, who do not through the day perform half a day's work. . . .'

"The reasons for discontinuing this system he [Commissioner Beattie] gives in his answer to our letter of inquiry (p. 119), and further in his conversation with us (pp. 34 and 35 of Appendix).

"Briefly summarized, they are: want of coöperation by the executive and finance departments; and vigorous opposition, open and secret, on the part of men interested in public life and desirous of holding public office." (He means the political power which held him and his men under close subjection.)

"The plain truth is that the system is of so long standing and of such sturdy growth that the right of appointment on the labor-roll of the department has come to be considered in some quarters a vested right; and no one who has not practical experience in such matters can conceive the tremendous resistance brought to bear against any effort to abolish or even to modify it.

"In our judgment, a radical change in the system of the employment of labor is imperatively demanded as the first condition of successful management of the department."

The question "What is the proper amount to be paid per month for labor?" was very carefully considered.

"On this point the committee has made somewhat extended investigations, inquiring as to rates paid by almost all the large corporations and private firms and individuals engaged in industrial enterprises in this city and employing a large force.

"Averaging the results obtained from answers to these inquiries, we find that the driver of a single truck or vehicle commands $10 per week wages, of a double vehicle $12 per week.

"This includes care of his horse or horses, and involves continuous duty from 6:30 A. M. in summer, and 7 A. M. in winter, until very frequently so late an hour as 9 P. M.

"Stablemen receive $40 a month. Car-drivers on surface roads, $2 a day for twelve hours' duty, of which ten hours is actual work on their platforms.

"Porters in employ of the large express companies, $50 per month. But these are exceptionally intelligent men, must possess special geographical knowledge of the continent, and work very long hours, frequently from 6 A. M. till 10 P. M.

"Porters on ordinary employment, $1.50 per day.

"Employees of railroad companies:

Track-laborers	$1.60 per day
Ashmen	1.50 " "
Coal-tenders	1.60 to $1.90 per day
Engine-wipers	1.50 " 1.75 " "
Sand-tenders	1.50 per day
Car-cleaners	1.50 to $1.90 per day
Deck-hands on steamboats	30.00 to 35.00 per month and board
Yardmen	1.25 per day
Flagmen	1.50 " "
Watchmen	1.50 to $1.75 per day

"The day, as here quoted, comprises from ten to twelve hours' work.

"On the 'L' roads:

Guards	$1.50 to $1.85 per day
Gatemen	1.25 to 1.75 " "

"It will be seen, from the instances above cited, that no class of unskilled labor commands the same rate of wages which is paid to the laborer working eight or ten hours per day by the Street-Cleaning Department. Taking twenty-six days' labor to the month, the city pays $52 per month for eight hours' work per day, and $65 per month for ten hours'.

"The current market rate for unskilled labor per hour in private business is at the rate of 12½ to 18 cents per hour. In comparison with these rates, the rates paid by the department are on an extravagant and wasteful scale."

As a conclusion from its investigations, the committee recommends a uniform rate of $40 per month for the laboring-force, which, in its judgment, would command workmen of the best class.

Its general conclusion is this:

"With good labor, skilfully organized and properly superintended, the streets can unquestionably be kept clean. With labor employed on the present methods, no organization, however skilful, and no superintendence, however faithful, can produce entirely satisfactory results."

As to the violation of the laws and ordinances relating to public cleanliness, the committee says:

"If the existing laws and ordinances regulating the conduct of householders and citizens with respect to cleanliness were faithfully observed and duly enforced, the task of the Street-Cleaning Department would be greatly lightened. The provisions of these statutes are full and ample, and seek the accomplishment of the following objects:

"1. Provision of suitable receptacles for ashes and

garbage, strong enough to contain the material without leakage or permitting the escape of any of it.

"2. Restriction of the amount of material to be placed in each receptacle, the limit of filling allowed being a line four inches below the top of the vessel.

"3. Forbidding interference with such receptacle by any persons not for that purpose authorized.

"4. Keeping the entire area of the sidewalk between the curb and the stoop-line free from these receptacles by prescribing the space between the stoop-line and the house-line of the premises as their proper location.

"5. Absolute prohibition to all persons to place any ashes, offal, vegetables, garbage, dross, cinders, shells, straw, shavings, filth, dirt, or rubbish of any kind whatever in any gutter, street, lane, alley, or any place in the city. Even shaking and beating of mats, carpets, and clothes in the streets is forbidden.

"The laws and ordinances in question issue from three sources—the Legislature, the Common Council, and the Board of Health; and for a wilful violation of any of them punishment by fine and arrest is prescribed, thus bringing the offenses within the class of misdemeanors. In addition to this, an offender against the Sanitary Code is liable to pay a penalty of $50 in a civil action to be recovered in the name of the Health Department.

"Theoretically, under the operation of these laws, New York should be one of the cleanest cities in the world; practically, it is one of the dirtiest, because they are so habitually violated and so feebly enforced as to become dead letters. . . . As a matter of fact, many of the gutters are choked with ashes and garbage, and piles of this offensive material can be seen in the streets themselves, which, if left uncollected for a few days, become in the winter season solidified masses resisting the action of any instrument less effective than a pickax, and frequently remaining undisturbed for a period of months. In our observation of the streets during the last eight weeks we have rarely found in the tenement districts any proper provision of suitable receptacles for ashes and garbage. We have seen the curbs of the sidewalks lined with boxes, both of wood and paper, broken barrels, small tin cans, and every conceivable unfit receptacle for ashes and garbage, all overflowing into the gutters. In addition to this, we have observed large piles of ashes and garbage thrown directly into the gutter, and upon the street itself, in default of any receptacle whatever. When we have seen a regular and proper receptacle for ashes, it has been in instances where it is evident that but one has been provided for a house containing many families, and consequently utterly incapable of holding the amount which must daily be gotten rid of. . . .

"But the violation of these ordinances is by no means confined to the tenement-house district. The law against throwing litter and rubbish of any kind into the gutters and streets is daily and hourly violated in the best sections of this city, and that by people who have not the excuse of ignorance of the law. We have seen prominent business houses on Fifth Avenue engaged in unpacking large cases upon the sidewalk, the operation involving the throwing into the street of paper, straw, and litter of all descriptions. We have seen well-dressed men on their way down-town deliberately toss into the public highway the eight-page newspaper which they had just finished reading. We have seen the same class of people disembarrass themselves of handfuls of paper and scraps by the same easy process. We have seen men engaged in repairing the sidewalks, where the material taken up was decayed wood, throw the debris into the public streets, and leave it there in piles. We have seen in front of a well-known and reputable establishment on Union Square the remains of a large awning, partially destroyed by fire, cast deliberately into the gutter. It is a matter of daily habit with many storekeepers upon the lines of the great lateral avenues to commence the day by sweeping out all the refuse litter of their stores into the streets.

"It is useless to multiply these instances; every one will recognize the fact of their daily and hourly occurrence. It is a hopeless task to keep the streets of this city clean so long as the people themselves are determined to keep them dirty. . . .

"We have in many instances seen offenses of the nature above specified committed under the eyes and the placid inspection of members of the police force. We have called the attention of the patrolmen to these violations and requested them to enforce the law. We have been met with manifestations of genuine surprise and the remark that when the people got through making the dirt they would probably clean it up by and by.

"The truth is that the authorities have so long acquiesced in this state of things that a large majority of the residents of New York are unaware of the existence of these laws, and in committing the acts described are unconscious that they are infringing them.

"More than this, we believe that many of the regular police force share this ignorance, and that an examination of the force, if fairly conducted, would show a large percentage of them unable to give an intelligent statement of the laws in question.

"The police magistrates of the city also fail to do their part in the enforcement of these ordinances. In many instances they have been known, instead of praising the efficiency of an officer who has brought offenders against the sanitary laws before them, to severely reprimand him for exceeding his province. When they impose a fine, it is apt to be the lightest allowed, and they are prone to treat cases of this kind with such levity that the offender is more apt to repeat the offense than to take warning."

CLEANING BY HAND OR BY MACHINERY

"The street-cleaning as conducted prior to the past year has been accomplished entirely by machines, a machine of the small pattern, drawn by either one or two horses, being used to brush the dirt into the gutters, where it is collected in piles by men with brooms and hoes, and these piles are shoveled into carts and removed to the dumping-boards. . . . The method of cleaning by machine has been extremely unsatisfactory, partly due to the bad condition of the pavements, partly to the difficulty of the machines getting through streets owing to the obstructions by trucks, and partly owing to a lack of proper supervision of their work."

FINAL DISPOSITION

The committee made the following report on the final disposition of the matters collected:

"The ashes and garbage and street-sweepings, collected in carts in the manner heretofore described, are taken to the dumping-boards, of which there are ten on each river. These dumping-boards consist of a rude platform eight to ten feet higher than the street, alongside of which lies a scow. The loaded carts are hauled up onto the dumping-board by the aid of a hill-horse, and the load is dumped in the open air onto the scow beneath. The material is then picked over by organized rag-pickers, who pay the city about $57,500 per year for the privilege, which is sold at auction. In this picking a small amount of material is dropped overboard, which in the aggregate soon becomes a large amount and requires frequent dredging of the slips alongside the dumping-boards. When a scow is loaded, it is taken away by a tug, and discharged either at sea or along the Harlem River, or other low grounds that require filling."

THE COST OF THE WORK

"The annual appropriations for conducting the business have varied from $1,010,000 in 1882 to $1,280,525 in 1890, the total for nine years ending with 1890 being $10,244,725. For the current year the appropriation is $1,584,250, of which $73,000 is for special police and $200,000 for new plant, leaving $1,311,250 available for cleaning, or about two per cent. more than in 1890. The accounts of the department are kept under seven different heads, and the expenditures for each in 1890 were as follows:

Administration . . .	$118,986.82,	or 9	per cent.
Sweeping	321,559.36,	" 25	"
Carting	528,768.63,	" 42	"
Removing snow and ice .	42,460.85,	" 3	"
Final disposition of material	235,816.09,	" 19	"
New stock . . .	16,539.00,	" 1	"
Rentals and contingencies .	15,517.09,	" 1	"
Total . . .	$1,279,647.84,	or 100	per cent.

"The expenditures varied per month from $83,776.66 in August to $124,999.59 in January.

"This sum of more than a million and a quarter of dollars, however, by no means represents the total amount expended for street-cleaning and removing refuse. . . . The total amount . . . expended from private funds to supplement the public service cannot be accurately stated, but we have the data to show that it is at least $100,000. Through the kindness of Mrs. Francis P. Kinnicutt, Mrs. Richard Irvin, and other ladies, who have made a careful canvass of the district between Eighth and Eightieth streets in the center of the city, we learn that not less than 2852 families in that district employ private ashmen, at an average of $2 per month, or a total of $68,448 per year. How much is expended in fees to public ashmen we cannot state, and it is even possible that householders sometimes mistake the public ashman for one supposed to be exclusively in their employ. This is exclusive of the large hotels, apartment-houses, and clubs, as well as shops and manufacturing establishments, all of which haul their ashes to the dumping-boards at their own expense. In this same district, not less than 63 blocks, with an aggregate length of about eight miles, are cleaned throughout the day on the patrol system at private expense, the price paid being about $500 per year for each block, or $31,500 in all. This is exclusive of Broadway, Fourteenth and Twenty-third streets, which are kept perfectly clean at the expense of the owners of large retail stores, at an estimated annual cost of $7000. These figures account for about $107,000 of private money expended for street-cleaning and removal of ashes and garbage, exclusive of what is spent by hotels and other large establishments above mentioned. What the total amount is we are unable to say, but there is reason to believe that it is between $150,000 and $175,000.

"We think it unnecessary to comment on this state of affairs further than to say that a system which leads householders to expend so large a sum of their private money, in addition to the taxes on their houses, in order to secure the measure of cleanliness to which they think they are entitled, is a system which leaves much to be desired on the score of efficiency."

The committee paid special attention to the standing of trucks in the street, condemning the practice, as have all who have had occasion to consider it, setting forth thus the practical difficulties which had been encountered in the experimental work they had done:

"The practical difficulties in the way of cleaning the streets when they are incumbered by vehicles are many and serious. In the experimental work done by the committee they were conclusively demonstrated. In the case of machine-sweeping, the machine was compelled to make a detour around every vehicle, averaging six feet in width and sixteen feet in length, leaving thus a hundred square feet along the gutters untouched. Where there was a wagon in front of each lot, the space between the wagons was too small to admit of a sweeping-machine working in toward the curb, and so a strip at least six feet wide from the curb-line was left unswept by the machine, rendering it necessary to follow the sweeper by a gang of men who had to move the vehicles and sweep the space beneath them by hand. Where trucks lined the street on both sides, as was frequently the case, over half the roadway, and that the more important part of it, had been left unswept. And since this was not an occasional occurrence merely, but a constant condition of the streets during the hours when the cleaners were at work, there had resulted an accumulation of street refuse under the trucks and carts of formidable proportions. Many of these vehicles, known as 'dead trucks,' have occupied the same space for a continuous number of years. The condition of the streets beneath them can readily be imagined.

"Where the cleaning was done by hand the difficulties encountered in the presence of the vehicles in the street were quite as imposing. To get at the pavement and gutters under the vehicles, the sweepers were required to move them out from the gutters and back again; and to do this required, in many instances, the utmost exertions of two or three men. Where the vehicles were few and far between, this was not a very serious matter; but instances of this description were so few that they do not materially affect the rule. The general rule is that there are so many vehicles, and that they take up so much of the street, that it would be impossible for the cleaners to regularly move them, and therefore the portion of the street occupied by them remains unswept. In the sections of the city where this rule most largely obtained, the accumulations of decaying and fermenting vegetable and animal matter had been undisturbed for weeks and months at a time, except as an occasional shower of rain had served to wash some of them into the sewers, and except where a truck or cart on leaving its mooring distributed a portion of them out over the pavement.

"The presence of these vehicles in the street, furthermore, renders exceedingly difficult the collection of ashes and garbage. Where the scavenger and ashman were required to move the ash- and garbage-barrels and other receptacles around long rows of wagons before they reached the cart into which they were to be dumped, it was inevitable that the sidewalks and streets should be littered with their contents, and that the work should reflect the carelessness of the men who were required to perform this unnecessary labor. From the sidewalks this refuse would be tracked into the houses and courtyards, pervading everything, and making cleanliness and order in the home next to impossible.

"The storage of these thousands of vehicles in the street is to be condemned not only because they make the regular cleaning of the street impossible, but because they are lurking- and hiding-places for the vicious and dissolute, the scenes of petty crimes and misdemeanors."

The committee's experiment was conducted during four weeks. It is worthy of very careful consideration, because it resulted in the introduction of the patrol or block system now in vogue.

"During the first two weeks, ending February 28, ice and snow prevented cleaning on three days, and the cleaning was in progress on nine days. On March 2 the sections were reversed, i. e., the machines were sent into the section which had previously been cleaned by hand, and vice versa; but a heavy snow-storm, followed by freezing weather, prevented making a fair test of cleaning on the third week. On the fourth week the weather was fairly good, and both systems were in full operation. In addition to almost daily observation of some portion of each district, we made a careful inspection of every street in both sections on February 23, and again on March 14. In the first inspection we found the hand-work, with a few trifling exceptions, well done; the streets were remarkably clean. But in many places we found the push-carts filled and a number of piles of dirt in the gutters awaiting the arrival of carts, showing that the cart service was defective. The machine section was not clean. The dirt had only been partially removed by the machines. In many streets the windrows of dirt in the gutter had not been heaped up, and in other streets large and numerous heaps of black mud had been left in the gutters for at least forty-eight hours. In our second inspection (March 14) we found the streets in both sections thoroughly cleaned, except where storekeepers had thrown refuse after the sweepers had stopped work; there was not a heap of dirt to be seen in the gutters anywhere in the entire thirty-two miles. The hand section was perfectly clean; the machine section was as clean as machines operating over rough pavements could possibly make it. There was a vast improvement over the work of two weeks before, and it was due to the fact that on March 12 Commissioner Beattie issued a positive order to his superintendent to employ enough carts to remove the sweepings every two hours in the hand section, and within one hour from the time the machines passed in the machine section; and this order was followed up by the commissioner, his deputy, and the superintendent passing the greater part of the next two days on the streets, supervising the work.

"This experiment clearly established certain facts, viz.: that with the patrol system, supplemented by a well-organized carting service, the streets can be kept perfectly clean at all times; that with machines the streets can be kept much cleaner than they have ever been kept before, provided the sweepings are promptly removed by an efficient carting service; that there are difficulties connected with the use of machines in this city, due to narrow, obstructed, and badly lighted streets (the work with machines must necessarily be done at night) and the uneven surface of the pavements, which make it impossible to clean the streets by this method as thoroughly as by hand; and finally, that in cleaning the streets by machine there is no provision for taking up the manure dropped during the day; the street may be perfectly cleaned at 7 A. M. and yet be very dirty at 9 A. M. and throughout the rest of the day from the accumulation of manure.

"We are therefore convinced that the patrol or block system of cleaning by hand is the best, if not the only, method by which the streets can 'be thoroughly cleaned and kept clean at all times,' as the statute requires."

GARBAGE

GENERAL OBSERVATIONS

BY C. HERSCHEL KOYL

THE subject of the final disposition of garbage is a municipal question; for with the single family or the small community all table and kitchen waste is valuable and eagerly sought as food for domestic animals. When fresh and wholesome, this is its proper and natural destination. It is only when, in larger communities, public health requires the banishment of the omnivorous hog that the disposition of putrescible waste becomes a question.

The early history of the subject, in all but seaport towns, is practically the same. The method of disposition adopted must be satisfactory at once to the community and to its neighbors. In seaport towns it has usually been cheapest and easiest to tow and dump the mixed wastes so far from shore as to be practically unobjectionable.

Inland towns, however, have commonly endeavored to sell their edible waste, even if not very fresh, to persons who hauled it away for use as food in large piggeries. Many, too, even within recent years, have used it in a partially decomposed condition as food for milch cows. But the consumers of the milk and the consumers of the pork have gradually risen in protest, and the guardians of health have urged many reasons why the practice should be abolished. The revenue derived from it and the difficulty of finding a better method have been serious obstacles to change; but the practice has generally given way to the compost heap, which, in turn, has usually died an early death from the vigorous objections of its neighbors.

A mechanical solution of the question then appeared the most promising. The first impulse naturally was to *destroy* an article which had given so much trouble; the second impulse was to *save* a substance which was known to be valuable. The development of these two ideas has led to the invention of crematories and utilization methods.

All new processes are liable to failure from inexperience and from the natural timidity of capital. Ear y attempts to destroy and to save this kind of city was e were defective in both cases, because no one quite knew what was needed, and every one hesitated to invest money which might be lost. The history of the past few years is therefore strewn with wrecks of laudable attempts to solve the problem.

The conditions of permanency and successful operation differ so much in different cities that an intimate and detailed knowledge of individual cases is necessary to an intelligent judgment of the inherent value of any particular process. In some places the relatively dry character of the waste and the mildness of the winter climate have permitted the easy and continued operation of crematories which, when called upon to burn wetter material, to maintain hotter fires, and to withstand the rigors of a Northern winter, have not sustained their reputation. In other places the location of a crematory or of a reduction plant has been so unwisely chosen that slight odors, or even the daily sight of a line of garbage-carts, has been enough to cause great complaint. Among the early reduction plants a fruitful source of trouble and failure was the tendency of enthusiasts to overestimate the amount and value of grease and tankage to be recovered, and thus to enter into unprofitable contracts, which both disheartened stockholders and prevented improvements suggested by experience. In many places, too, the municipal authorities have been so divided in opinion that the small majority by which a system has been introduced has not been able to withstand the trifling criticisms which would have passed unnoticed had the company been longer in operation or backed by a stronger popular desire for its success.

Only careful examination by experienced judges, and extended over a reasonable time, can give any accurate idea of the accomplishment or possibilities of such a process. Many of the difficulties to be overcome have now been learned by experience, and have been briefly discussed above. They are primarily hygienic, secondarily economic, and all are nearing solution.

In the case of the smaller cities whose outskirts are easily reached, and in many of which combustible waste is mixed with kitchen refuse, crematories have been established and are in use, with results more or less acceptable. The later installations, with their improved methods, are, of course, better than earlier ones.

In Wilmington, Delaware, the Brown crematory has been used; in New Brighton, Staten Island, Terre Haute, Indiana, and Gainesville, Texas, the Brownlee furnace; in Allegheny, Pennsylvania, the Rider; in Camden, New Jersey, McKeesport, Pennsylvania, Atlanta, Georgia, Fort Wayne, Indiana, and Salt Lake City, the Dixon; in Lowell, Massachusetts, Coney Island, New York, Richmond, Virginia, Savannah, Georgia, and in numerous places, principally in the South and West, the Engle; in Atlantic City, New Jersey, Philadelphia, Muncie, Indiana, etc., the Smith-Siemens; in Scranton, Pennsylvania, the Vivarttas. Many other towns have purchased and operated other crematories, with varying success.

Among the larger cities, Buffalo, New York, with a population of about 300,000, pays $35,000 per year to the Merz Company to receive and dispose of its garbage by a reduction system; Detroit, Michigan, with 250,000 population, pays annually $63,000 for collection and disposal by the same process; Milwaukee, Wisconsin, with 250,000 people, pays $24,000 for disposal by the Merz Company; and in St. Louis the Merz Company receives and reduces all garbage and offal at $1.80 per ton.

Cincinnati, with 350,000 population, and payment on a sliding scale averaging about $22,000 per year, and New Orleans, 250,000 population, send their garbage to plants of the Simonin utilization system. In this process garbage is spread upon crates and, within closed iron cylinders, subjected to the action of naphtha and steam heat until the grease and water are extracted, after which the dry matter may be culled and ground.

In Philadelphia, where "slop" is collected and disposed of by contract, many methods have been in successive or contemporaneous use. At present all the "slop" which is treated within the city limits goes either to one of the two Smith crematories or to the large reduction plant of the Arnold system.

Chicago, too, has tried nearly every known method, and is still experimenting—just now with crematories.

Boston, which has always derived a revenue from the sale of "swill" to neighboring feeders and towed the balance of its waste to sea, made a contract some two years ago with a local company operating the Arnold process; but the plant was closed after a few months' operation, and now the city has temporarily returned to its ancient method.

Washington, D. C., has had a somewhat similar experience, except that the Arnold plant was destroyed by fire, and, owing to the uncertain condition of the contract then in force, it was not rebuilt. The health officer of the city has lately made an extended visit to plants in operation in other cities. This is one of the places where something *must* be done, and it is said that recent contracts have been made for the erection of two crematories, one of which is already completed.

Pittsburg operated for years an overworked and unsatisfactory crematory, and the present contractor has lately built a reduction plant in which it is proposed to manufacture the garbage dry matter into a complete fertilizer. The method in use is that of the Consolidated American Reduction Company.

Cleveland, hampered by poverty, has done little yet, but hopes to put a reduction plant into operation in the near future.

New York and Brooklyn are pressed by necessity to an early decision.

C. H. K.

HISTORY OF THE GARBAGE CONTRACT IN NEW YORK

BY MACDONOUGH CRAVEN

THE following extracts from a paper giving a short history of the bids, etc., in relation to the final disposition of the city's wastes, can best be introduced by the letter of April 9, 1896, which was supplied to the leading daily newspapers:

April 9, 1896.

DISPOSAL OF THE CITY'S WASTES

After the contract for the disposal of garbage goes into effect, new methods will be adopted for the treatment of all our wastes. Some of them are already inaugurated, and all should be in full use before the end of the year.

1. Garbage will be kept separate, in such vessels as the Board of Health may prescribe, and will be collected by special carts.

2. Ashes and dust (free from paper and other rubbish) will be kept within the house, or in the back yard, in special cans. From these they will be removed in tied bags by department men, who will stand them on the edge of the sidewalk.

3. Street dirt will be placed in a bag (carried on a light truck) as fast as it is swept up. When the bag is

filled it will be tied and stood on the sidewalk. This system has been in use in Madison Avenue since last summer, and is now being extended.

The ash-carts will move slowly along the streets, with enough men attending to throw the bags into them as they pass. Thus the shoveling of sweepings and the emptying of receptacles, as well as the standing of receptacles on the streets and the collecting of sweepings into piles, with their attendant dust, litter, and nuisance, will be forever done away with.

4. All refuse other than garbage, ashes, and dust will be kept within the house until called for by the department "paper-carts," which will remove everything the householder wants to get rid of, from an envelop to a mattress or a cooking-stove. These things will be taken to central depots, where everything of salable value will be separated, and all else will be cremated.

When this system is in complete operation, not only will the streets be clean, but they will also be tidy. Blowing papers and the dust nuisance will have disappeared. Furthermore, the $80,000 hitherto received by the city for the privilege of picking bones, bottles, rags, etc., during the trimming of the scows, will be replaced by many times that amount received for the much larger quantity of material collected, and collected in much better condition. There are further possibilities as to the use of unsalable paper for pasteboard, the development of steam for power by the burning of refuse, the use of ashes for making brick- and concrete-work; but concerning these we are not yet in a position to make any public statement.

The obtaining of information as to articles of possible value which are now practically thrown away, and which might be recovered and sold, has involved an expenditure on the part of the city, in the form of scow-trimming money received by Herbert Tate since June 17, 1895, of $57,225. Of this, $6150 has been paid as compensation to Herbert Tate and his assistants for the installation and management of the investigation; $480 for rent of the lot where the crematory stands, at the corner of

Fifty-third Street and Twelfth Avenue; $5800 for the construction of the crematory and appurtenances; $1339 for the operation of the crematory. There stands to the credit of the crematory account about $1350 received for paper, bottles, shoes, etc., sold.

The remainder of the sum received has been used for the employment of carts and trucks, varying in number from 41 to 79, and averaging 54 per day. Believing always that the experiment was to last but a few months, collection was made from all parts of the city below Fifty-ninth Street, and irregularly above Fifty-ninth Street, with a view to preventing the people from putting their paper and rubbish into the streets. This has had a good effect—by no means a complete effect. The material collected in the fifth district, being between Twenty-second Street and Fifty-eighth Street and from Sixth Avenue to the Hudson River, together with a portion of what was collected above Fifty-eighth Street was delivered at the crematory, foot of Fifty-third Street, and wasmade the subject of the experiment referred to above.

There has been a doubt in the minds of some persons as to my authority for applying the scow-trimming money to this use. The case was presented in all its details to the counsel to the corporation, Mr. Scott; and he not only said that I had the right to use the money in this way, but that he thought it would be well worth while to find out whether or not there was a possibility of getting a greater value out of the wastes of the city than it was then receiving.

The experiment would have been concluded last autumn had the plan been carried out at that time of asking proposals for the treatment of garbage. By request of the mayor, this plan was changed, and, on terms and conditions approved by the Board of Estimate and Apportionment, an advertisement was published asking for proposals for the disposition of all of the wastes of the city. The bids under this proposal were opened December 10, 1895, without result.

The next advertisement asked for proposals for disposing of garbage alone, at a fixed price per ton. This was dated January 22, 1896; the bids were to be opened February 4, but the time was extended to February 17 for readvertising. This also was without result.

Again, on March 12, 1896, we advertised for proposals for the removal of garbage alone, at a per annum price, the bids to be received up to March 26.

March 17, proposals were asked for the disposition of ashes, sweepings, garbage, etc.; these were to be received March 30. Both sets of bids were opened on March 30, 1896. These proposals are now under consideration.

As soon as the decision of this question allows us to resume the even tenor of our way, we shall make ready to close up our experimental work, and go forward with our plans for handling all of our output in the manner set forth.

A false start was made in April, 1895, with Walton & Co., but, after they had used $1667.90 of the scow-trimming money, the arrangement was found not to be satisfactory and it was canceled.

George E. Waring, Jr., *Commissioner.*

The long and difficult proceedings through which the final result was reached are fully set forth in a paper published by the department. This will be sent to those who apply for it. It is not without interest, but there is no room for its details in these pages.

At the last meeting of the Board of Estimate and Apportionment at which the matter was discussed, the mayor offered the following:

"*Resolved*, That the Board of Estimate and Apportionment hereby approves the report of the commissioner of street-cleaning, dated May 1, 1896, stating that he has rejected all bids for final disposition, except that of the New York Sanitary Utilization Company, and the said board hereby approves of the contract with the said New York Sanitary Utilization Company, recommended for acceptance by said commissioner of street-cleaning, as to its terms and conditions, including the price or compensation therein provided for."

The president of the Board of Aldermen moved as a

substitute that "this board declines to approve of the bid of the New York Sanitary Utilization Company as recommended by the commissioner of street-cleaning."

The chairman put the question whether the board would agree to said substitute, and it was decided in the negative by the following vote: Affirmative: the president of the Board of Aldermen—1. Negative: the mayor, controller, president of the Department of Taxes and Assessments, and counsel to the corporation—4.

The question recurring on the original resolution as offered by the mayor, it was adopted by the following vote: Affirmative: the mayor, controller, president of the Department of Taxes and Assessments, and counsel to the corporation—4. Negative: the president of the Board of Aldermen—1.

On June 6, 1896, the contract was entered into with the New York Sanitary Utilization Company, and preparations were immediately made for beginning the work.

M. C.

NOTE.—This contract was for five years. The city pays an annual compensation of $89,990. It delivers the garbage on the contractors' vessels, which take it to Barren Island, at the mouth of Jamaica Bay, where it is cooked for ten hours by steam (under a pressure of seventy pounds). It is then pressed, the grease is taken from the liquid and made ready for market, and the solid matters are dried and prepared for use as manure.

The arrangement is advantageous to the city and profitable to the company.

INDEX